REKINDLE YOUR LOVE FOR JESUS

Rekindle Your Love
for Jesus

DAVID E. ROSAGE

CHARIS
Servant Publications
Ann Arbor, Michigan

Charis Books is an imprint of Servant Publications especially designed to
serve Roman Catholics.

Published by Servant Publications
P.O. Box 8617
Ann Arbor, Michigan 48107

Cover design: Hile Illustration & Design, Ann Arbor, Michigan

96 97 98 99 00 10 9 8 7 6 5 4 3 2 1

Printed in the United States of America
ISBN 0-89283-932-5

Library of Congress Cataloging-In-Publication Data

Rosage, David E.
    Rekindle your love for Jesus / David E. Rosage.
        p. cm.
    ISBN 0-89283-932-5
    1. Jesus Christ—Devotional literature.   2. Retreats.
3. Spiritual life—Catholic Church.   4. Catholic Church—
Doctrines.   I. Title.
BT306.5.R67   1996
232—dc20   96-515
                                                         CIP

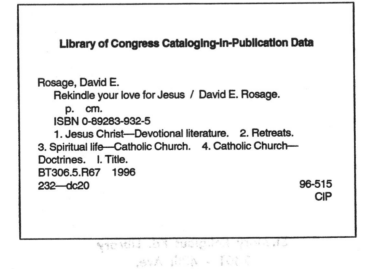

Contents

Acknowledgments

I am eternally grateful to all those wonderful people who led and encouraged me on my journey to a more personal relationship with Jesus.

I am grateful to all the retreatants who patiently listened as I tried to share some of these thoughts with them, and for their constant urging to commit them to writing.

I wish to thank two special friends who helped me very much in the preparation of this book: Mary Krone, who typed and retyped this manuscript in many ways and forms, and Emily Ehlinger, who spent much time in editing the text.

INTRODUCTION

AT THE BEGINNING OF THE FIRST MILLENNIUM of Christianity, St. Paul apprised his pupil Titus of his hopes and expectations of the years ahead and exhorted Titus to proclaim this message "in season and out of season."

> For the grace of God appeared, saving all and training us to reject godless ways and worldly desires and to live temperately, justly, and devoutly in this age, as we await the blessed hope, the appearance of the glory of the great God and our savior Jesus Christ, who gave himself for us to deliver us from all lawlessness and to cleanse for himself a people as his own, eager to do what is good.
>
> **Titus 2:11-14**

As we enter the third millennium, there would be no reason for Paul to change one iota of his exhortation. As we recommit and rededicate ourselves to a deeper, more fervent Christian way of life, the Lord's presence and power, his gifts and graces, are with us enabling us to "reject godless ways and worldly desires and to live temperately, justly and devoutly in this age."

To bring St. Paul's message into our present-day Christianity, Pope John Paul II published an Apostolic Letter, *As the Third Millennium Draws Near*. This letter designates the triennium 1997-99 as a time of concerted preparation for the desired fruits of the Third Millennium. In his letter the Pope listed some of the anticipated fruits:

> Everything ought to focus on the primary objective of the Jubilee: the strengthening of the faith and of the witness of Christians. It is therefore necessary to inspire in all the faithful a true longing for holiness, a deep desire

for conversion and personal renewal in a context of ever-more intense prayer and of solidarity with one's neighbor, especially the most needy (#42).

The Pope has designated the first year of the triennium (1997) as a time to focus on the Person of Jesus and to establish a deep, personal relationship with him. Contemplating Jesus as a personal, loving, providing, forgiving and healing Lord will transform us and elicit within us a loving response to him.

Those who call themselves *Catholic* or *Christian* but have never entered into relationship with Jesus himself are missing out on a vital source of spiritual life. Following only those religious practices that are convenient, or striving to adhere to each letter of the law through actions that are devoid of real devotion results in a lifeless imitation of real faith. On the other hand, cultivating a loving relationship with the living Christ will vitalize religious "practices" and fill our lives with the sense of purpose and meaning for which there is an almost universal yearning.

Rekindle Your Love for Jesus has been prepared to meet and respond to that yearning. The Person of Jesus is central throughout this book. In each chapter we meet Jesus as he asks us a direct question about our knowledge and understanding of him, or challenges us to listen to him with our whole being. He longs to enlighten us about his own mind and heart. Only when we know the heart of Jesus are we able to love him. Lovers strive to imitate and meet the expectations of the person loved. The axiom "we become what we contemplate" is verified in our relationship with the Lord.

Each of the eight sections in this volume contains two complementary chapters. In the first chapter, Jesus asks a provocative question: "What do you seek?" (John 1:38). He intends his direct question to encourage us to examine our understanding of him and our personal relationship with him. In the following chapter, Jesus reveals more about himself: "I am the light of the world" (John 8:12). Reflecting on this self-revelation should bring us to a deeper awareness of his abiding presence with us and also keep us always aware of his loving concern for us. In some sections the procedure is reversed: Jesus first states something about himself in an "I AM" passage and then asks his question in the next chapter.

The content of each chapter is not simply to be read for information, but to be the source of our reflection and prayer. Our quiet listening and honest response to him will draw us into a personal union with him. Select one chapter for each day's prayer. Recall it at some time throughout the day, and, at the close of the day, review it once more. This process will have a powerful transforming effect upon us, enabling us to grow and mature spiritually to become the people the Lord expects us to be.

A number of questions are arranged at the end of each chapter that will help us review our relationship to Jesus.

In a brief exhortation, Pope John Paul II said, "The great tragedy of history is that Jesus is not known, is consequently not loved, not followed. You know Christ! You know who he is! Yours is a great privilege! Know how to be always worthy and conscious of it!"[1]

With the inspiration and guidance of the Holy Spirit, may the following pages assist us in reaching a personal, loving, peaceful, joyful relationship with Jesus, our Lord, our Master, our Teacher.

CHAPTER ONE

"What Do You Seek?"

IF YOU WERE INVITED TO ACCEPT a certain position or undertake a leadership role in an organization, your first question would probably be, "What does this position entail?" or "What are your expectations of me?" You could even use the words Jesus addressed to the disciples of John the Baptist who were following him after his baptism in the Jordan: "What do you seek?" (Jn 1:38).

When Jesus was about to begin his public ministry, he went down to the Jordan River and asked to be baptized. John the Baptist introduced him to the crowds in these words: "Behold the Lamb of God, who takes away the sin of the world!" (Jn 1:29). To appreciate all the nuances of this scene, we need to listen with our hearts to the gospel account of this episode.

> The next day again John was standing with two of his disciples; and he looked at Jesus as he walked, and said, "Behold, the Lamb of God!" The two disciples heard him say this, and they followed Jesus. Jesus turned, and saw them following, and said to them, "What do you seek?" And they said to him, "Rabbi," (which means Teacher), "where are you staying?" He said to them, "Come and see."
>
> **John 1:35-39**

JESUS LEAVES A LASTING IMPRESSION

When we meet an important person or experience some major event in our lives, we remember not only the place where we were but even the time of the day. Spouses happily recall the day and place they first met each other and what impression it left on them. Likewise, a person who wins a new car in a raffle will doubtless remember the day and place he was when he received the news.

In the same way, when we experience the Lord's presence in our lives at a particular moment, it leaves a lasting impression on us. We will not readily forget the place and circumstances of this God-given experience.

When the two disciples of John met Jesus for the first time, they were deeply impressed by him. One disciple, Andrew, went off to call his brother Simon Peter. The other unnamed disciple was probably John, who recorded this meeting in his Gospel. He remembered this event so clearly that years later he related the exact place (on the banks of the Jordan) and the precise time (about 4:00 in the afternoon).

With his introduction, "Behold the Lamb of God, who takes away the sin of the world," John was really proclaiming Jesus as the long-expected Messiah, for only God can take away sin. Naturally, the two disciples were eager to get to know more about Jesus. Was he really the Messiah? What was he like? What was he teaching? How did he hope to accomplish his mission?

As the disciples followed Jesus, he surprised them when he turned and asked, "What do you seek?"

"Rabbi, where are you staying?" they must have stammered. Jesus invited them, as he does us, saying, "Come and you will see." This was not merely an invitation to see where he was staying, which was probably in a goatskin tent provided for pilgrims along the Jordan. Rather, Jesus was inviting them to come and listen to what he was teaching, to observe his way of life. They were eager to know if he was going to call disciples to follow him and what he expected of them. Primarily, Jesus wanted them to realize what kind of Messiah he was.

Jesus' question to the disciples—"What do you seek?"—was an important one. Many Jews of that day had false expectations about the Messiah who was to come. Some were hoping for a strong military leader who would free them from the domination of Rome; others were awaiting a powerful political leader who would restore the glory of the Davidic golden age. Still others longed for a Messiah who, according to the prophecies, would redeem them from their sinfulness and bring them eternal glory.

WHAT DO WE EXPECT OF JESUS?

Still today people often have false notions about the role of Jesus in their lives. Some regard him as one of the great prophets, a marvelous social reformer or a masterful teacher, but not as a divine Savior and Redeemer.

Others think of Jesus as an impersonal deity, off in his glory far removed from the concerns that they face every day. They do not realize that the Lord dwells with them and within them, and is vitally concerned about their feelings, cares and problems. They are unable to see how he assists them with the duties and demands of each day.

Those Christians who know Jesus as a loving, gracious God are aware of his presence abiding with them, loving them, inspiring them, strengthening them at every moment of the day. They try to keep themselves aware of his presence as they journey down the pathway of life.

Imagine Jesus here and now with us asking the same question he asked the disciples of John: "What do you seek?" Such a direct question arrests our attention, causes us to pause and ponder, and inspires us to reflect on our relationship with him.

Such soul-searching will help us to review our attitudes and actions, and will lead us to contemplate the Person of Jesus. As we consider prayerfully this important question, Jesus will reveal more about himself to us. And as we come to know him as a compassionate, loving God who is deeply concerned about us at every moment of the day, it will enlighten us to respond to this outpouring of his love.

We cannot love a person we do not know. Nor can we know a person to whom we have not listened with our hearts. As we prayerfully listen to Jesus, his kindness, mercy and compassion will unfold and enkindle within us a deeper love and appreciation of his goodness to us. These deeper insights into his gracious personality will enable us to respond more honestly and sincerely to the question he poses to us: "What do you seek?"

FINDING GOD IN PRAYER

We all have different expectations when we go to God in prayer. Some people talk to God only when they want something from him, and expect him to be at their "beck and call." Others need the constant reassurance of his presence, and feel disappointed when they don't constantly feel it. Still others doubt God's loving concern when their prayers aren't answered at the time and in the manner they wish.

As we come to know God more intimately, we adjust our attitudes in this regard. We become less self-centered and more Christ-centered. We come to trust that even when our prayers aren't answered the way we want them to be, God's love and care for us do not change. We rely on the promises the Father gives to us in Jeremiah:

Then you will call upon me and come and pray to me, and I will hear you. You will seek me and find me; when you seek me with all your heart. I will be found by you, says the Lord, and I will restore your fortunes.

Jeremiah 29:12-14

IS GOD JUST A "PORT IN THE STORM"?

"God is in his heaven, all is right with the world," wrote Robert Browning. Do you sometimes feel that you don't want to "bother" God with "small" problems? Many people never think of asking the Lord's guidance and help until their best-laid plans fall flat. Until problems strike, we are apt to forget the caution Jesus gave us: "Apart from me you can do nothing" (Jn 15:5).

Failure is good therapy, keeping us humble and ever aware of our dependence on the Lord. It reminds us that the Lord is eager to assist us at every moment of the day if we let him. We need to remind ourselves that this is a divine promise and that God is a faithful God. Jesus also assures us of the power of prayer and his response to our petitions.

Ask, and it will be given you; seek, and you will find; knock, and it will be opened to you. For every one who asks receives, and he who seeks finds, and to him who knocks, it will be opened.

Matthew 7:7-8

Coming to prayer with this divine reassurance will enable us to respond to Jesus when he asks, "What do you seek?"

"YOUR FAITH HAS HEALED YOU..."

During his earthly sojourn, Jesus' healing love touched everyone who came to him in faith. He is in his glory now, but what is his glory? His glory is continuing his healing mission among us. How often we stand in need of his healing power!

When anxieties, worries and frustrations come our way, we need his inner healing to allay our fears, doubts and misgivings. When physical aches and pains visit us, especially those illnesses which force us to suspend our daily plans and activities, we need to remember that these painful experiences can heal and mature us in other areas of our lives. Suffering and pain can be our stepping stones on our journey heavenward. St. Augustine tells us that no evil can befall us from which the Lord cannot derive some good. The power of God's healing love will generate a calm, peaceful acceptance of our suffering which will greatly mitigate its severity.

Jesus heals us spiritually by helping us to overcome our self-centeredness, our lack of love for others and other undesirable weaknesses. In his merciful, compassionate love, he forgives our many faults and sins. When Jesus asks, "What do you seek?", our reflection brings us to realize that he is continually healing us physically, emotionally and spiritually. How often with a grateful heart we should whisper a fervent "Thank you."

When Jesus asks us, "What do you seek?" we may wish to ask him for genuine peace of mind and heart. He would remind us that he is the Prince of Peace and that he will always be faithful to his farewell promise to us: "Peace I leave with you; my peace I give you. Not as the world gives do I give it to you" (Jn 14:27). Prayerfully basking in the sunshine of his unconditional love will bring us much peace.

JESUS, WHAT DO YOU SEEK IN ME?

What a revelation it would be for us if we had the courage to rephrase the question, asking Jesus instead, "What do you seek in me?" Would we dare to ask Jesus, "Am I meeting all your expectations?" As we think about this question, we must guard against a false sense of security ("Of *course* I'm doing all God could expect!") or condemnation ("I could *never* please God with my life").

As we spend time patiently and prayerfully listening to the voice of Jesus in our hearts, we discover that as our shortcomings loom up in our minds, there is no reason for discouragement or disappointment. As we rest in his presence, we are reminded that Jesus is a patient, loving God who knows all our weakness and waywardness, all our hopes and desires, all our faults and foibles, all our endeavors and trials.

As you rest in his abiding presence, visualize him laying his hand upon you and saying, "Regardless of what you have done, or not done, I love you anyway." Recognizing his boundless love will help us to be humble and honest in facing all our willfulness and shortcomings, and make us more resolute in trying, with his help, to overcome them. This is what the Lord expects of us—our honest effort.

Naturally we build high expectations for ourselves. We want to be loved and appreciated; we want to succeed in all our endeavors; we want to be respected and acknowledged. Somehow we never quite reach the expectations we have set for ourselves. However, there is no reason to become disheartened or discouraged. The Lord knows our humanness and looks only at our intentions. He is pleased when we extend mercy to others when they disappoint us, and when we honestly and sincerely strive for worthy ideals.

❧❦

For Reflection

Jesus wants us to focus on our expectations of him in order to ascertain how closely our heart, mind and will are in tune with his.

- Is Jesus for me a "port in the storm"? Do I run to him only when problems, difficulties and hardships come my way?

- When I pray am I disappointed and discouraged if I do not feel his presence? Do I become easily frustrated when my prayers are not answered immediately or in the way I expect them to be?

- Do I expect Jesus immediately to dispel all my worries and anxieties and to heal my aches and pains? Do I consider uniting my sufferings along with his for the salvation of souls?

- Do I have enough courage to ask Jesus: "What do you seek in me?"

- What is one memorable moment that I can recall in my own relationship with Jesus?

CHAPTER TWO
꧁꧂

"I Am the Light
of the World."

WHEN JESUS ASKED THE DISCIPLES of John the Baptist "What do you seek?" he invited them to "come and you will see." Jesus wanted them to visit with him and to learn firsthand about him and his mission. He likewise invites us to come to him that we may know more about him.

When Jesus asks us, "What do you seek?" he does so to encourage us to make an inventory of our expectations of him. What do we really want of him? Are our expectations conducive to our spiritual welfare, or are they, at times, unreasonable, mundane and self-centered? To enable us to focus on genuine expectations, Jesus makes some direct statements about himself that reveal a great deal about his personality through his attitudes, his words and actions:

> I am the light of the world; he who follows me will not walk in darkness, but will have the light of life.
>
> **John 8:12**

In Scripture, light is always symbolic of the presence of God; darkness portrays the sinister aspects of evil. Jesus, the Light of the World, is a recurring theme in John's Gospel. In the introduction John writes, "The true light that enlightens every man was coming into the world" (Jn 1:9).

When Jesus declared himself the Light of the World, he was assuring us that he would enlighten our understanding, enabling us not only to discern good and evil, but also to comprehend more fully his enduring love for us. In his Letters, John repeatedly mentions the struggle between light and darkness, between good and evil, but always with the assurance that Light will overcome darkness.

Jesus promises us that he will always be with us to guide and direct our course heavenward. As the Light of the World, Jesus is like a lighthouse on our journey through life. He guides and illumines our pathway as we live each day. When all is calm, peaceful and uncluttered in our life, Jesus is like a lighthouse on a clear, calm day. On such a day, we admire the beauty of a lighthouse adorning the landscape. It is there to offer us security and safety and to give us a sense of confidence and reassurance. However, when life becomes stormy and ill winds prevail against us, we welcome the comforting beams of the Lighthouse to guide us through the storm-tossed waves and wind.

KEEPING OUR FOCUS

When Peter wanted to venture out of the boat onto the water to meet the Lord, all was well until he encountered the raging wind and waves. In panic he called out, "Lord, save me" (Mt 14:30). Take note that Peter did not try to return to the boat but cried out to Jesus to rescue him.

In the same way, we need Jesus when the way is dark, foggy and obscure. We need the comforting Light of Christ when our horizon is dimmed by pain, discouragement or grief. We need the encouraging Light of Christ and his comforting presence to broaden our human perspective. His love replaces our sadness with joy, our discouragement with hope. He is the Light beckoning us to the entrance of the tunnel. What assurance his words give us: "As long as I am in the world, I am the light of the world" (Jn 9:5).

LIGHTS IN THE WINDOW

An artist took great pains to paint a picture he envisioned. It was a wintry scene with a little cottage nestled in a grove of fir trees. The snow lay heavily on the branches of the trees and on the roof of the cottage. It was night and the scene was dark and dreary. The artist stood back, studied his work for a long time, then stepped forward and, with a few deft strokes, put a light in all the windows of the cottage. The whole scene was immediately transformed into one of glistening beauty.

Just as the light from the windows of the cottage, reflecting on the white snow, gave the whole picture a new glow, so also the Light of Christ brings a new brilliance to the world enmeshed in sin. Once our world, too, was dark and dismal, enmeshed in the hideous darkness of sin and evil. When Jesus came into the world, the whole scene was changed. Hope and peace penetrated and dispelled the darkness of sin. The prophet foretold this transformation:

> The people who walked in darkness,
> have seen a great light;
> Upon those who dwelt in the land of gloom
> a light has shone.   **Isaiah 9:1**

We recall the redemptive act of Jesus dispelling the darkness of sin and bringing light into our sinful world during the Easter vigil. As the procession moves into the church with the newly lighted paschal candle, the priest or deacon chants three times, "Light of Christ." The people joyfully respond, "Thanks be to God."

LEAD, KINDLY LIGHT

John Henry Newman's search for a loving, personal God led him from Calvinism into the Anglican Church where he was ordained a priest in 1835. After a few years he became disenchanted with some of the theology and practices of the Anglican church, forcing him to set out on another agonizing search which eventually brought him into the Roman Catholic church and into the priesthood and later the cardinalate.

During his wearisome struggle with doubts, fears and uncertainties, he sought the Lord's guidance by imploring him as the "Light of the World." He poured out his heart to the Lord seeking the enlightenment he needed to know and follow his divine will.

It was during this period of searching that he was inspired to compose his widely known poetic prayer, "Lead, Kindly Light." As the Light of the World, Jesus will illumine our pathway on our journey through the turbulent waters of life. And we, as did Cardinal Newman, will find great hope and peace in the prophecy of Isaiah: "The Lord will be your everlasting light" (Is 60:19).

The Light of Christ is not merely a tiny, flickering flame; his brilliance outshines the sun. Without the sun, no life could exist on our planet. Without the Light of Christ, our spiritual life could not survive. The Light of Christ, like the sun, lifts our spirits and gives us hope and encouragement when fears, doubts, anxieties and frustrations arise. Just as the rays of the sun penetrate a forest of trees, so the Light of Christ searches us out when we are inundated with countless, often mundane concerns.

We find inner peace. The Light of Christ becomes a deep and abiding presence within us. As we learn to rest and relax in him, we experience the peace and tranquility that only the Lord can give. The hassles and worries of the day cannot disturb us when we focus in quiet prayer upon our Lord.

Vincent and Mary, like many other parents, were distraught and deeply disappointed when their sons and daughter strayed away from the sacramental life of the church. When they shared their pain and disappointment with me, I tried to offer them hope and encouragement by assuring them of God's unconditional love for their children. I explained that he has his arm around them and would continue to pursue them.

Then I urged them to pray in a particular way for themselves and their straying children. To help them enter into this method of prayer, I suggested a number of passages in the Bible revealing the enduring love of the Lord, such as the parables of the Lost Sheep and the Prodigal Son (see Luke 15) along with several others. I encouraged these good parents to pray with confidence and trust, and let the words of the Lord find a home in their hearts, assuring them that they would certainly find comfort and a peace which the world cannot give. Jesus really meant it when he promised, "Come to me, all who labor and are heavy laden, and I will give you rest" (Mt 11:28).

We discern God's will for ourselves more readily. The Light of Christ enlightens us to discern not only God's ordinary will, but his will of preference in all the events of daily living. It will help us make the right decisions in all the perplexities of life.

As we try to discern what the Lord is asking of us in a given situation, we can often sense through circumstances or within our spirits what he intends for us to do. This might be compared to a traffic light which orchestrates the flow of vehicles by the illumination of multicolored lights.

At times we may encounter a "red light." It may be a

physical restraint or impediment to our actions, or simply an "inner sense" that we should stop and consider our plans more carefully. On other occasions we may experience a delay or feel compelled to slow down, much as a yellow light slows oncoming traffic. At still other times we may sense a "green light" when we are inspired to proceed with our intended course of action, assured of our Lord's blessing and guidance. What a blessing to know Jesus as the Light of the World!

We learn to avoid situations that cause us to stumble. I always enjoy landing at an airport at night. It is so reassuring to see the blue lights outlining the landing strip. Likewise, the powerful landing lights on the plane illumine the runway clearly so that the pilot can bring the plane down for a safe landing.

The Light of Christ is always before us, illuminating our minds and hearts and escorting our footsteps safely through the maze of mundane allurements. The effectiveness of the light is determined by the degree to which we are receptive and cooperative in permitting it to enlighten and guide us. Sin not only dims the light but can cut it off completely, forming an opaque veil, as it were, between us and the Lord. Its effects are devastating. Sin darkens our minds chills our hearts, weakens our faith and cools our love. It threatens to decimate our relationship with the Lord. However, if we make an effort to raise the curtain, the light will be there to flood our soul once again. Jesus promised, "I am the light of the world; he who follows me will not walk in darkness, but will have the light of life" (Jn 8:12).

The Light of Christ guides us in all our human relationships. If we walk into a darkened room and turn on the light, we do not gaze at the light. The function of the light is to reveal certain relationships: the relationship between the footstool and my shin, between my foot and the first riser of the stairs.

Christ's Light illumines the way to love our neighbors as ourselves. His Light will highlight the good in others. As the Light of the World, Jesus also reveals our relationship with our loving Father. He assures us that the Father loves us with an infinite love—a love which is caring, concerned, forgiving and enduring. This awareness elicits a loving response of appreciation and a willingness to fulfill his will in our lives by doing whatever pleases him. His Light guides us in our relationships with all those who come into our lives. It enables us to see and appreciate the worth of each person more clearly. His Light helps us establish genuine Christlike relationships with our neighbors.

HIS LIGHT, OUR RESPONSE

The Light of Christ abides with us constantly. It is not like a bonfire which blazes brilliantly but is soon burned out. Jesus is the enduring Light, illumining our path throughout all the labyrinthian ways of our earthly sojourn. He promised never to leave us: "Lo, I am with you always, to the close of the age" (Mt 28:20).

Jesus promised to be with us at all times as the Light of the World, but we must be willing to be receptive and permit his light to guide us as we journey. We could react to his light in various ways.

- We may totally ignore his Light and launch out on our own.

- We may move away from the Light, relying primarily on our own resources, seeking his way only when "emergencies" arise.

- We may turn to the Light, basking in it and being guided by it.

JESUS COMMISSIONS US

After Jesus fills us with his light, love and peace, he commissions us to bring his light to all those we meet along life's pathway. He reminds us, "You are the light of the world" (Mt 5:14). This is a great compliment, revealing the trust and confidence the Lord has in us. As the Light of the World, Jesus assures us that since we have accepted his way of life and have put on his mind and heart, we, too, are lights in the world:

> Let your light so shine before men, that they may see your good works and give glory to your Father who is in heaven. **Matthew 5:16**

Our good deeds are not so much the feverish activity that we engage in to help others as an opportunity to radiate Christlike concern by our attitudes and dispositions. We bring light to others by the peace and joy of our hearts shining forth in all our interpersonal relationships. In this way we are mounting our light where others may see it (see Luke 8:16).

瘤瘤

For Reflection

Jesus is the Light that beckons us to follow so that he may brighten our day, guide our footsteps and illumine our minds and hearts. He also fills us with his light that we may be a light to others. Ask yourself:

- Are there parts of my life I prefer to keep hidden in darkness, not allowing Jesus to shine his Light into that area?

- Am I apt to attribute my good deeds to my own ingenuity rather than acknowledge that God enlightens and empowers me in all my endeavors?

- When I perform a good deed, do I await the expressed gratitude and appreciation of others, even though Jesus cautions me, "Do not let your left hand know what your right hand is doing" (Mt 6:3)?

- Do I depend on the Light of Christ to enlighten me in establishing Christian relationships with everyone who comes into my life?

CHAPTER THREE

"Who Do You Say That I Am?"

THE TIME WAS RAPIDLY APPROACHING when Jesus was to go to Jerusalem to face his enemies, to be condemned and to lay down his life for our salvation. He was well aware that his disciples and other followers would be shocked and scandalized; some would even seriously doubt his divinity.

For this reason, Jesus took his disciples away from the crowd to a sparsely populated area at Caesarea Philippi. In this secluded area he tested them and wanted them to express their faith in him regardless of what was to come.

> Now when Jesus came into the district of Caesarea Philippi, he asked his disciples, "Who do men say that the Son of man is?" And they said, "Some say John the Baptist, others say Elijah and others Jeremiah or one of the prophets."
>
> **Matthew 16:13-14**

When Jesus first asked the disciples, "Who do men say that the Son of man is?" the disciples dutifully reported the various opinions they had overheard in the synagogue, among the crowds in the marketplace and in other gatherings. They passed this information on to Jesus without disparaging or endorsing it.

Most people were not sure who Jesus was. Some thought he might be John the Baptist risen from the dead, or Elijah. Still others were of the opinion that he was Jeremiah or one of the prophets. Among people today there are likewise various and sundry opinions about Jesus and the role he plays in our life.

Jesus, the law-giver. Unfortunately there are some people who regard Jesus as an exacting law-giver setting forth rules, laws and regulations by which we must live: "Love your neighbor as yourself.... Love your enemies.... Take up your cross daily...."

With this mentality, these directives will seem a burdensome restriction of personal freedom. Without the proper motivation and understanding, we too might have formed these attitudes. Those who do not know Jesus personally will usually find his way of life a great burden.

Jesus, the safe haven. Many people who rarely think of the Lord when all is going well do not hesitate to run to him immediately when problems and difficulties arise, when illness and suffering plague them or when worry and fear beset them.

This realization of their dependence upon the goodness of the Lord and a sincere crying out for his help is a prayer posture. It pleases the Lord when they recognize him as a faithful companion walking ever at their sides. He never abandons them, even though they may forget to prayerfully express their thanks and appreciation for his providential care.

Jesus, the forgiving God. People more readily recognize their need for the Lord when a sense of guilt and sinfulness overwhelms them. Throughout his ministry Jesus manifested his eagerness to heal and forgive everyone who came to him with a contrite heart.

When people seek his mercy and forgiveness, it pleases our Lord, who wants to be known as a compassionate and forgiving God. He wants to forgive sinners more than they could want it themselves. When G.K. Chesterton converted to Catholicism, a friend asked him what prompted him to become a Catholic. He responded in these few words: "To have my sins forgiven." He too could respond to Jesus' question, "Who do you say that I am?"

The transcendent Jesus. Some people visualize Jesus in all his celestial glory and imagine that he has little concern for their daily struggles. They are unaware that Jesus makes himself so immanent that he is living with and within them at every moment of the day. They are oblivious to his divine promise made on several occasions. "If a man loves me he will keep my word, and my Father will love him, and we will come to him and make our home with him" (Jn 14:23). He reiterated his promise the night before he died: "I will not leave you desolate; I will come to you" (Jn 14:18). In his farewell to the disciples, he reminded them again, "Lo, I am with you always, to the close of the age" (Mt 28:20). With these words Jesus enables us to respond to his question, "Who do you say that I am?"

JESUS PROBES DEEPER

Jesus was not content to hear his disciples reiterate what they had heard "through the grapevine." He wanted his disciples to express their own personal opinion of him, so he zeroed in on them: "But who do you say that I am?"

We can well imagine some moments of hesitation and silence as they glanced around at each other before Peter spoke up. He could have formulated his answer in words such as: "You are the eschatological manifestation of the ground of our being, the kerygma in which we find the ultimate meaning of our interpersonal relationships and of the trinitarian, authentic and ecclesial mysteries."

Although the statement would have been correct, it would not have said a great deal about Peter's heartfelt attachment to him. Is our understanding of Jesus mostly intellectual, making Jesus a sort of theological definition? Or do we want to know him with our hearts as a loving, personal God?

Here is Peter's actual response to Jesus' question:

> Simon Peter replied, "You are the Christ, the Son of the living God." Jesus answered him, "Blessed are you, Simon Bar-Jonah! For flesh and blood has not revealed this to you, but my Father who is in heaven...."
> **Matthew 16:16-17**

Jesus explained that the Father had blessed Peter with the gift of faith, which enabled him to recognize Jesus as the Messiah and Lord. Peter's faith in Jesus also enabled him to know Jesus with his heart as a loving, gracious God, and not merely as an abstract theological entity. Jesus asks each one of us, as he did the disciples: "But who do you say that I am?" To respond honestly will require some prayerful reflection.

WHO DO YOU SAY JESUS IS?

Visualize Jesus placing his hand on your shoulder and looking into your eyes as he asks, "Who do you say that I am?" An honest response will require some instant soul-searching. We may have a good knowledge of christology and be aware that he is the second Person of the Blessed Trinity, co-equal and co-substantial with the Father and the Holy Spirit. We may be aware of the two natures in Jesus, and also have some knowledge of the other mysteries surrounding him. Such knowledge is intellectual and can bring us to understand Jesus theologically, but it does not bring us to an appreciation of his mind and heart.

In our consumer-oriented society we readily judge people by what they can accomplish. Seldom do we judge them by their attitudes, dispositions and personality. In the same way, our first inclination may be to appraise Jesus by what he has done for us, rather than marveling at his boundless love that prompted these actions. We must know Jesus with our hearts and not merely with our heads.

LEARNING TO LOVE JESUS WITH OUR HEARTS

When Jesus asks us, "Who do you say that I am?", we may be startled by such a direct question. How would we respond? Do we try to remain aware of Jesus' constant presence loving us, assisting us, motivating us, encouraging us? Would we detect his presence with us if he stood beside us at this very moment? "If a man loves me, he will keep my word, and my Father will love him and we will come to him and make our home with him" (Jn 14:23).

How would we recognize Jesus? Nowhere in the Gospels do we find a word picture of his physical appearance. We have no idea if he was tall or short, light-complexioned or swarthy, thin or stocky. His sojourn on earth was in the pre-camera days, no 35mm, no camcorders.

In the Gospels, however, we do find a clear delineation of his personality. Jesus revealed his mind and heart to us as he spoke and went about doing good. As we spend time with him in reflective prayer, we will come to appreciate his caring and concern, his forgiving and healing love. As we contemplate the Person of Jesus, he will reveal very much about himself, which we could not otherwise know. Thomas Merton reminds us that contemplation gives us insights beyond analysis. Praying contemplatively will give us insights that we could not otherwise have about Jesus.

THE POWER OF CONTEMPLATIVE PRAYER

The contemplative (or reflective) prayer posture may be compared rather mundanely to taking a sunbath. All that is required of us is to place ourselves in the sunshine, rest and relax there. The sun will do all the rest. It will warm us, nourish us, cheer us.

Similarly, God's love and his presence rejuvenates us. As we rest in the sunshine, so we rest in his presence and love, thus permitting him to mold and transform us. In a little booklet entitled *Simple Prayer,* Carmelite Sister Wendy Mary Beckett prepares us to enter into the prayer of listening with our hearts in these few words: "The essential act of prayer is to stand unprotected before God. What will he do? He will take possession of us...."[1]

A mundane example may bring us to an appreciation of coming "unprotected before God." Imagine a dry sponge dropped into the ocean. The sponge will immediately absorb all the water it can hold without changing the water level of the ocean. When we are dropped into the ocean of God's love, he fills us to the saturation point with his love, thus taking possession of us.

Every time we meet Jesus in the Gospels, he reveals more and more about his personality and his human and divine concern for us. According to St. Theresa of Avila, in order to become a prayerful person, we must know the human Jesus. In Scripture, we discover the human Jesus:

...who gets hungry and thirsty (Jn 4:7-8)
...who hugs lepers (Lk 5:12ff)
...who eats with sinners and tax collectors (Lk 15:2)
...who becomes angry at hypocrisy (Mt 23:13ff)
...who feels lonely and deserted (Mt 26:36ff)
...who weeps at the loss of a friend (Jn 11:35)
...who mourns over the fate of Jerusalem (Lk 9:41)
...who heals the sick and the suffering (Lk 9:11)
...who walks on the water and calms a storm (Mt 14:22)
...who multiplies loaves and fishes (Mk 6:34ff)

Scripture assures us that the Lord's mission of love remains unchanged for us today, for "Jesus Christ is the same yesterday, today and for ever" (Heb 13:8). In our reflective prayer, we will become more aware of the loving care and concern of Jesus:

...who walks with us at every moment of the day,
...who picks us up when we stumble and fall,
...who holds our hands when we are afraid,
...who smiles at us when we reach out in loving concern for others,
...who sits beside us when we pray,
...who waits for us to join him in offering the Eucharist,
...who blesses us at the close of the day,
...who loves us so much that he is eagerly waiting to share the bliss, joy, peace and happiness of heaven with us.

The more time we spend regularly and consistently in prayer contemplating the personality and lifestyle of Jesus, the more we will become like him. We become what we contemplate, as St. Paul informs us: "And we all, with unveiled face, beholding the glory of the Lord, are being changed into his likeness from one degree of glory to another; for this comes from the Lord who is the Spirit" (2 Cor 3:18).

But there is yet another important question we need to ask ourselves. If Jesus would come to visit with us at this moment, would we be embarrassed? Are our lifestyles and our thinking so totally in conformity with his will that we would feel no discomfort whatever? Are our thoughts and attitudes always so in tune with the mind and heart of Jesus that we would experience no sense of guilt, no uneasiness, no reason to excuse ourselves or to ask for forgiveness?

❧❧

For Reflection

To respond adequately to Jesus when he asks, "But who do you say that I am?", we need to spend some quality time in surveying our own attitudes, dispositions and reactions throughout the course of each day. Only then will we be able to respond to his searching question.

- Do I try to keep myself aware that Jesus is my constant companion living with me and within me at this very moment?

- Do I return frequently to the Gospel with renewed interest, listening to what Jesus reveals about himself?

- Do I strive to capture the sentiments and feelings of Jesus as he ministers to the poor and downtrodden, to sinners and to those who are sick and suffering?

- Do I rest and relax regularly in his presence, permitting his Word to find a home in my heart that it might transform me into the kind of person Jesus wants me to be?

CHAPTER FOUR

"I Am the Way, and the Truth, and the Life."

WHEN JESUS ASKED HIS DISCIPLES "Who do you say that I am?" he knew that they did not fully understand him or his mission, nor did they suspect that his redemptive death was approaching quickly. When Peter made his profession of faith, Jesus reminded him that it was his heavenly Father who inspired him to acknowledge Jesus as "the Christ, the Son of the living God" (Mt 16:16).

When Jesus asks us "Who do you say that I am?" he realizes that there is, and always will be, great mystery surrounding him. For this reason Jesus gradually reveals more and more about his mind and heart as we prayerfully follow him throughout the Gospel narrative.

Each time Jesus speaks in the Gospels, he tells us more about himself. He reveals his heart and personality through his words, his actions and attitudes, and by his care and concern for every person he encountered. He also reveals an aspect of his divine personality in what is commonly called the "I AM" passages:

"I am the Good Shepherd."
"I am the Light of the world."
"I am the bread of life."

He reveals an additional aspect in the "I AM" passages upon which we are reflecting in this chapter in his final discourse at the Last Supper.

"Let not your hearts be troubled; believe in God, believe also in me. In my Father's house are many rooms; if it were not so, would I have told you that I go to prepare a place for you? And when I go and prepare a place for you, I will come again and will take you to myself, that where I am you may be also. And you know the way where I am going." Thomas said to him, "Lord, we do not know where you are going; how can we know the way?" Jesus said to him, "I am the way, and the truth, and the life; no one comes to the Father, but by me."

John 14:1-6

When Jesus proclaimed himself "the way, and the truth, and the life," he was using a phrase familiar to the Jews. However, they had always associated it with Yahweh or God. They did not grasp that they would find the fulfillment of this proclamation in Jesus and his teaching.

"I AM THE WAY...."

Moses had already admonished his people to walk in the way of the Lord: "You shall be careful to do therefore as the Lord your God has commanded you; you shall not turn aside to the right hand or to the left. You shall walk in all the way which the Lord your God has commanded you" (Dt 5:32-33).

Moses' words to the Jewish people (and to us) reminded them of the fundamental importance of remaining on the straight and narrow way, of swerving neither to the right nor to the left. The psalmist prayed in the same vein:

"Teach me thy way, O Lord; and lead me on a level path" (Ps 27:11).

The role of Jesus as the Way has a threefold dimension: his teaching, example and presence.

The teachings of Jesus. Jesus was a teacher par excellence. In the Gospels he taught us by words, admonitions and parables. His discourses outline the truths by which we are to live if we are to be his followers.

When we travel to an unfamiliar part of the country, we need a road map to guide us along the best route. After carefully studying the map, we set out along the way indicated to reach our destination. As our teacher, Jesus gave us the road map for our otherwise uncharted journey through life to our eternal home.

As our teacher, Jesus followed the accustomed method of teaching in his day. Since writing materials were scarce, Jesus, like the rabbis, summarized the essence of his teaching in a short prayer or poem. In this way the hearers committed to memory a core idea that enabled them to recall other facets of the teaching.

The very heart of Jesus' teaching and his way is love. Hence he taught his disciples: "You shall love the Lord your God with all your heart, and with all your soul, and with all your mind. This is the great and first commandment. And a second is like it, you shall love your neighbor as yourself" (Mt 22:37-39).

Only when we love are we following Jesus and his way.

The example of Jesus. Jesus' whole lifestyle is a perfect pattern that we are challenged to emulate. On one occasion Jesus advised his disciples and us, "For I have given you an example, that you also should do as I have done to you" (Jn 13:15). In another instruction he told us what was necessary for following him as the Way: "A new commandment I give to you, that you love one another; even as I have loved you, that you also love one another" (Jn 13:34). When we strive to love one another, we are following his way.

The presence of Jesus. Jesus fulfills the third dimension of his role as the Way through his abiding presence with us and within us. His presence, uniting our spirit with his, is dynamic, encouraging and strengthening us at every moment of the day. He illumines our path when we are hesitant and fearful, when the hills seem high and the valleys deep, when we are perplexed and under strain. What reassurance his words bring us: "Lo, I am with you always, to the close of the age" (Mt 28:20).

In his farewell address, he promised to return in his new and exalted life to remain with us: "I will not leave you desolate; I will come to you" (Jn 14:18). Jesus is present with us not only to show us the Way, but to walk every step of the Way with us.

The Lord does not force us to follow his way; he waits for our response. St. Paul's urging is a direct imperative: "Put off your old nature which belongs to your former manner of life and is corrupt through deceitful lusts, and be renewed in the spirit of your minds, and put on the new nature, created after the likeness of God in true righteousness and holiness" (Eph 4:22-24).

Jesus leads the way. While it is true that Jesus *is* the Way, it is just as true that he is faithful to lead us *in* the way we should go. He accompanies us on our daily journey.

Imagine yourself in a strange city and uncertain about reaching your destination. If you ask a person for directions, he might graciously tell you, "Take the first street to the right and turn left at the next intersection past the church. Cross the square and then take the third street on your right and the street you are looking for should be on your left." Without a doubt you would be confused and lost before you traveled half the distance.

But suppose the person would say to you, "It is quite confusing, but follow me and I will lead you there." This is precisely what Jesus does for us. He does not simply give us directions and advice. He takes us by the hand and accompanies us, strengthening and encouraging us personally through the hours of the day. To be sure, he is the Way.

On one occasion, I went to a small town to visit the father of a priest friend. I had the street address but had no idea where I might find Virginia Avenue. As I entered the town, I saw a policeman sitting in his car. When I asked him how to get to this address, he asked, "Are you going up to see Wendell? Just follow me." Jesus does the same for us. He does not merely give us directions but he invites us: "Follow me, and I'll take you there." How appropriately he calls himself the Way.

"I AM... THE TRUTH."

When Jesus says, "I am... the truth," he does not simply mean that he is truthful and trustworthy. He is Truth itself. Truth is the sum total of all perfection. As the Truth, Jesus is the embodiment of all moral and spiritual truths, to which Christians must conform in order to have the mind and heart of Christ within them.

The psalmist prays for this kind of conformity to the truth: "Teach me thy way, O Lord, that I may walk in thy truth" (Ps 86:11). And again, "I have chosen the way of truth" (Ps 119:30, NAB).

Many people are meticulously honest in telling the truth at all times. In doing so, they are conforming to the concept of Truth which Jesus personifies. In this way they reflect a Christlike attitude. On our journey in life, Jesus urges us to conform our minds and hearts to him, the perfect Truth. He leads us along the path to Truth and empowers us to strive earnestly for this goal.

The Lord also calls us to a special mission to lead others in pursuit of the truth. Moral and spiritual truths cannot be taught solely by words. They are taught by example. To the extent that we faithfully follow Christ's example, our lives radiate his love and peace to everyone we encounter. A person's character may or may not affect the way he teaches a course in mathematics or the classics—primarily intellectual pursuits. But if a person proposes to teach a spiritual truth effectively, his lifestyle must conform to all the norms he is attempting to teach.

A teacher might give an eloquent and persuasive presentation on the negative effects of needless worry and undue anxiety, and immediately afterward push the panic button when some little difficulty arises. The effects of his or her teaching are then negated by the conflict between the teacher's words and actions. As we attempt to impart moral truth, the consistency of our example is critical. Jesus alone can say "I AM the Truth," but as we strive to imitate his lifestyle, we can reflect a shadow of that truth.

"I AM... THE LIFE."

Jesus says very plainly, "I am... the life." What a profound truth! What an astounding gift! Jesus was speaking not of physical life but of his own divine life that he had come to share with us by his redemptive sacrifice. A brief reflection on the history of salvation will give us a deeper appreciation of God's loving care for us.

When sin entered into the world, the human race severed its relationship with God, cutting off the divine life and intimate relationship it had enjoyed with God before the Fall. The resulting breach between man and God was so vast that there was no possibility of closing it by human means. Only the unbounded love of God could rebuild this severed relationship.

But the Father loved us so much that he sent Jesus into the world as our Redeemer to bring us his divine life: "For God so loved the world that he gave his only Son, that whoever believes in him should not perish but have eternal life" (Jn 3:16).

We are reminded of this truth again in John's first Letter: "In this is love, not that we loved God, but that he loved us and sent his Son to be the expiation for our sins" (1 Jn 4:10). Thus, in Scripture Jesus gives us the reason for his coming into the world: "I came that they may have life, and have it abundantly" (Jn 10:10).

Jesus accomplished his redemptive mission by taking on our unredeemed human nature so that he could take it down to death with him to redeem us, giving us the potential to receive his divine life. St. Paul explains this truth in these words when he asks:

> Do you not know that all of us who have been baptized into Christ Jesus were baptized into his death? We were buried therefore with him by baptism into death, so that as Christ was raised from the dead by the glory of the Father, we too might walk in newness of life.
>
> **Romans 6:3-4**

This newness of life is the divine life, the risen exalted life that the Lord shares with us at our baptism. The Lord asks us to be receptive to the life he wishes to share with us, permitting it to increase and develop within us. We are Christians because Christ's divine life dwells within us. He unites his Spirit with ours to energize us, to inspire and motivate us and to transform us by the "newness of life," enabling us to grow and mature in our Christian way of life. We are then able to reflect his love and peace to everyone we meet. Can there be any greater privilege than to have Jesus as *our way and our truth and our life?*

❧❧

For Reflection

In determining the status of our relationship with Jesus, we must ask ourselves, "How do I see Jesus as the Way and the Truth and the Life?" The following examination may help.

- Is my mind and heart always in tune with the heart and mind of Jesus who is the Way?
- Am I always truthful, honest and sincere in all my words and actions? Does my life reflect the attitudes and attributes of Jesus who is the Truth?
- Do I try to comprehend and appreciate the divine Life with which Jesus endows me, giving me my real dignity as a person?
- Do I enjoy his divine Life within me as a foretaste of the peace and joy awaiting me in eternity?

CHAPTER FIVE

"I Am the Good Shepherd."

A RECURRING IMAGE IN SCRIPTURE that focuses on the Lord's loving concern is the figure of a shepherd caring for his sheep. This image of a good shepherd immediately brings to mind the many splendors of God's love for us. One of the best known and loved psalms is Psalm 23, commonly known as the "Shepherd's Psalm." This psalm joyfully relates all the ramifications of the Lord's boundless love. Pray it reflectively.

> The Lord is my shepherd, I shall not want;
> he makes me lie down in green pastures.
> He leads me besides still waters; he restores my soul.
> He leads me in paths of righteousness for his name's sake.
> Even though I walk through the valley of the shadow of death, I fear no evil; for thou art with me; thy rod and thy staff, they comfort me.
> Thou preparest a table before me in the presence of my enemies....   **Psalm 23:1-4**

It was only after I had spent time in Israel leading a renewal program for African sisters that I appreciated all the nuances of this psalm. There I discovered firsthand the close relationship between a shepherd and his sheep.

"The Lord is my Shepherd...." Jesus says, "The sheep hear [the shepherd's] voice, and he calls his own sheep by name and leads them out" (Jn 10:3). To appreciate the significance of this statement, we need to recall that there was a common corral in each little village to house and protect all the villagers' sheep throughout the night. In the morning, when the shepherds came to lead their own sheep to pasture, they would call each one by name. Each sheep would immediately follow its shepherd, while the other sheep remained in the stockade. Watching this immediately brings to mind the Father's loving care: "I have called you by name, you are mine" (Is 43:1).

"He leads me beside still waters." The shepherd does not lead his sheep to just any watering hole but to restful waters where the sheep are not afraid to drink. One day when the Sea of Galilee was quite stormy and the high waves lapped the shore rather vigorously, I watched a shepherd carving out a basin to catch the water so that his sheep could drink without fear of the turbulent water. The Good Shepherd also reminds us that he will give us very special water—the "living water" of divine life. Jesus exclaimed: "If any one thirst, let him come to me and drink. He who believes in me, as the scripture has said, 'Out of his heart shall flow rivers of living water'" (Jn 7:37-38).

"He leads me in paths of righteousness for his name's sake." As our Good Shepherd, Jesus mapped out his way for us to follow during our earthly exile. His statement was direct: "I am the way, and the truth, and the life" (Jn 14:6).

While conducting a retreat on the Mount of Beatitudes, I enjoyed an excellent view of an Arab farm close by. Every morning when the corral gate was opened, the sheep came out to gambol and romp with the little children who screamed with delight. After some time an older boy, who was to shepherd the sheep that day, called out an order and the flock immediately fell in line as they followed him down the path and off to a grazing area. As I daily watched this performance, I thought of the Good Shepherd's invitation to his flock: "Follow me."

A woolly sheep can easily fall in the rugged terrain. With the crook of his staff, the shepherd can more easily help a sheep to his feet. In the same way, when we are weighted down by the burdens of life—the trials and tribulations that often overwhelm us—our Shepherd guides us in the way we should go. His familiar voice comforts us; his promises are sure.

"Thy rod and thy staff, they comfort me," is a guarantee of the Lord's protection as he guides us amid all the happenings of life. I watched some boys passing the time while they watched over their little flocks by tossing their shepherd's rods at various targets. They became so dexterous that they could injure or kill an animal that might threaten their sheep. Thus the Lord protects us.

The shepherd's staff is indicative of the Lord's providential care and guidance. The staff is not simply a walking stick; the crook is useful in guiding a sheep to a little patch of grass here and there, since their fields are not lush grazing ground. A sheep rarely looks up while grazing, and may not notice more food some distance away. How often do we get so caught up with the business of living that the Lord must prod us to feed our souls?

"Thou preparest a table before me in the presence of my enemies." In Scripture the table or a meal is often a reference to the messianic banquet in heaven where we, with the psalmist, hope to "dwell in the house of the Lord forever." How aptly the psalmist sums up the limitless, unbounded love of the Lord as Shepherd when he says,

"Surely goodness and mercy shall follow me all the days of my life" (vs. 6).

SHEPHERD LOVE IN THE OLD AND NEW TESTAMENTS

In the Old Testament, the Father assures us that as our shepherd, his providential love will supply all our needs, both of body and soul. Ponder his words as he tells us:

> I myself will be the shepherd of my sheep, and I will make them lie down, says the Lord God. I will seek the lost, and I will bring back the strayed, and I will bind up the crippled, and I will strengthen the weak, and the fat and the strong I will watch over; I will feed them in justice.   **Ezekiel 34:15-16**

In the New Testament we discover a popular and much loved portrayal of Jesus as the Good Shepherd that echoes the Father's assurances in the Old Testament. Jesus not only identifies himself as the Good Shepherd, but also reveals his loving concern for each of us, his sheep. His love blossoms out frequently in the Gospel under the image of the Good Shepherd as he preaches the Good News, curing every disease and illness.

And, as in the Old Testament, the people were much in need of that Good Shepherd. "When he saw the crowds, he had compassion for them, because they were harassed and helpless, like sheep without a shepherd" (Mt 9:36). Jesus brought comfort and reassurance to the little flock of his disciples. "Fear not, little flock, for it is your Father's good pleasure to give you the kingdom" (Lk 12:32). In numerous other ways he manifested his loving concern. Consider several lines from the Ezekiel passage in light of the message of the New Testament:

"I will make them lie down." In the New Testament, Jesus, the Good Shepherd, reaffirms the Father's promise when he invites us: "Come to me, all who labor and are heavy laden, and I will give you rest" (Mt 11:28).

"I will seek the lost." How comforting are the words of the parable Jesus used to reveal his deep love for the lost sheep (see Luke 15:1-7). The whole heavenly host celebrates with the Good Shepherd when a "stray" returns to the flock. "There will be more joy in heaven over one sinner who repents than over ninety-nine righteous people who need no repentance" (Lk 15:1-7).

"I will bind up the crippled and I will strengthen the weak." The psalmist joyfully reiterates the extent of the Lord's love: "Who forgives all your iniquity, who heals all your diseases" (Ps 103:3). Throughout his public ministry Jesus, our Good Shepherd, healed all who came to him with faith, regardless of their ailments. He always healed the whole person—body, soul and spirit. Clearly, shepherding is love in action; shepherding is divine love dynamic within us.

When Jesus identifies himself as the Good Shepherd, he reveals the many facets of love and concern for every one of us, his sheep. Jesus is the quintessence of all the admirable qualities of a good shepherd. He leads and guides his sheep. He provides for and protects them. He is vigilant and patient, and radiates his tenderness and compassion as he sets the lost sheep on his shoulders with great joy (see Luke 15:5). The direct statements Jesus makes about himself should convince us of his boundless love for us.

"MY SHEEP HEAR MY VOICE"

As the Good Shepherd, Jesus calls each of us by name. He knows us intimately and individually, as if each one of us were the only person in his care. We are pleased when someone calls us by name. It proves that person's concern for us. It is important to be recognized and appreciated. How gratifying to hear the Lord say, "Fear not, for I have redeemed you; I have called you by name, you are mine" (Is 43:1).

As the shepherd leads his sheep to grazing areas, they are docile in following him, trusting that he will find nourishment for them. Likewise, Jesus leads us forth each day by inspiring, enlightening, motivating and encouraging us to follow his way of life and put on his mind and heart.

Next Jesus tells us, "I am the good shepherd; I know my own and my own know me, as the Father knows me and I know the Father" (Jn 10:14-15). The word Jesus used, which is translated "to know" in English, means not only to know *about* a person but to know another person from the heart, to appreciate all that person's goodness, likes and dislikes, hopes and ambitions. Only when we know a person so intimately can we love him or her. Certainly the Father knows Jesus perfectly; Jesus, likewise, knows the Father. In other words, Jesus knows us better than we know ourselves. His love for us is infinite and unconditional.

As we spend time in wordless prayer listening to Jesus with our heart, he will reveal himself to us, bringing us into an experiential awareness of his abiding presence and love within us. Only when we know deep within ourselves that he loves us will our love for him blossom out more fully.

HOW WELL DO YOU KNOW JESUS?

The difference between knowing Jesus intellectually and knowing him with our hearts as the Good Shepherd was evident at a formal dinner in England. A noted actor had been engaged to do some Shakespearean readings. He received long and sustained applause for a masterful rendition of the great bard. He then asked if there were any requests. A rather shy priest asked the actor if he knew Psalm 23. He assured the priest that he did and would recite it on condition that the priest would do the same.

When the actor had finished, once again he received loud applause for his rendition of the psalm. As promised, the priest rose and recited the psalm as well. When the priest finished there was only a hushed silence—no applause. After some moments the actor stood up and said, "I know the psalm, but Father knows the Shepherd."

We, too, need to *know* the Shepherd rather than simply know *of* him.

JESUS, THE SHEEP DOOR

Jesus expands the image of the Good Shepherd when he says, "Truly, truly I say to you, I am the door of the sheep" (Jn 10:7). We need to be aware of the customs of that time to appreciate this figure of speech.

When a shepherd had to travel far from home to find good grazing ground, it was not always possible to take his sheep back home at night. In that part of the world there were numerous caves in the chalk hills. The shepherd would corral his sheep in one of these caves and then lie down at the entrance to prevent any wild animal from attacking his sheep. Likewise, no sheep would cross his body.

Jesus compared himself to the door, which was the person lying across the entrance of the cave. He assured us of his enduring protection when he said, "I am the door; if any one enters by me, he will be saved, and will go in and out and find pasture" (Jn 10:9).

THE SELF-SACRIFICING SHEPHERD

Jesus confirmed the extent and intensity of his love for us when he proclaimed:

> I am the good shepherd. The good shepherd lays down his life for the sheep.... For this reason the Father loves me, because I lay down my life, that I may take it again. No one takes it from me, but I lay it down of my own accord. **John 10:11, 17-18**

Jesus' redemptive death for our salvation was the total gift of himself, a gift freely given. This gift was the ultimate expression of his love. As Jesus himself noted, "Greater love has no man than this, that a man lay down his life for his friends" (Jn 15:13).

The Father loved Jesus for laying down his life, since the Father's sole desire was to have us united with him in heaven. Since our relationship with the Lord was severed when sin entered the world, the sacrificial death of Jesus, who had taken on our human nature, was the only means by which we could regain the eternal bliss of heaven. When Jesus said, "I lay down my life that I may take it again," he was creating a new and exalted life, which he shares with us that "we too might walk in newness of life" (Rom 6:4). In the Gospel of John, Jesus himself confirmed the purpose of his coming: "I came that they may have life, and have it abundantly" (John 10:10).

When Jesus identified himself as the Good Shepherd, he opened the floodgates of his divine love with all its intensity and ramifications penetrating every area of our earthly sojourn. Now he asks us, "DO YOU LOVE ME?"

❦

For Reflection

The following questions may help us to evaluate our relationship with Jesus, our Good Shepherd. Respond honestly and sincerely as he asks:

- Do you often reflect on my role as your Good Shepherd caring for you, guiding you, watching over you, protecting you, loving you?

- Do you really trust me when I tell you that I am your Good Shepherd caring for all your needs?

- How much do you appreciate the gift of faith I have given you? How thankful are you that I have called you to be a member of my fold?

- Are you deeply concerned for the other sheep that "do not belong to this fold"? Do you pray for them? Does your attitude reflect my love, peace and joy to them?

CHAPTER SIX

"Do You Love Me?"

In the popular movie *Fiddler On the Roof,* one scene depicts the family patriarch, Tevye, asking his wife, Goldie, an important question: "Do you love me?" Goldie hesitates and does not respond immediately. Tevye repeats his question: "Do you love me?" Once again Goldie does not give a direct answer, seemingly embarrassed by the question. He asks again. Finally, exasperated, she blurts out, "For twenty-five years I washed your clothes, cooked your meals, cleaned the house, gave you children and milked the cow and now you ask, 'Do you love me?'"

Tevye's question was an important one. Goldie needed to affirm her love for her husband, and he needed her to verbalize it. It was equally important for Tevye to declare his love for his wife and to hear himself expressing it in his own words.

"SIMON PETER... DO YOU LOVE ME?"

A somewhat similar encounter takes place in the closing episode of John's Gospel. The time of Jesus' earthly sojourn was drawing to a close. He was preparing the apostles for his departure from them and his return to his Father. In the twenty-first chapter of John, Jesus appeared to the disciples at the Sea of Galilee where they had gone fishing. After a long and tiresome night, they had caught nothing.

Jesus once again proved his loving concern for them as he stood on the shore and called out to them, asking if they had been successful in netting any fish. When they answered "No," he advised them to cast their nets on the right side of the boat. They did, and their catch was so great they could scarcely drag their nets to the shore.

After sharing a picnic breakfast with them, Jesus took Peter aside and asked him a vitally important question: "Simon, son of John, do you love me?" Such a direct question must have startled Peter for a moment, but his reply was reassuring: "Yes, Lord; you know that I love you." A second and a third time, Jesus asked the same question: "Simon, son of John, do you love me?" Finally Peter replied, "Lord, you know everything; you know that I love you."

Why did Jesus ask Peter if he loved him? And why did Jesus persist in asking Peter three separate times? Jesus knew that Peter loved him; otherwise, he would not have left home and his livelihood to follow Jesus. Surely this should have been a manifestation of Peter's love for the Lord. However, it was important for Peter to affirm his love for Jesus, and also to hear himself verbalizing it. The affirmation of his love would encourage and strengthen Peter for the task that Jesus would ask him to undertake.

Let us recall that this was not the first profession Jesus had exacted from Peter. A short time before, when Jesus was about to begin his ministry of suffering to redeem the human race, he took the apostles to Caesarea Philippi, away from the crowds. Jesus was well aware that many, including the apostles, would be scandalized by his suffering and crucifixion. Alone with them, he elicited a profession of faith from them, asking, "Who do you say that I am?"

Peter broke the silence and affirmed his faith in Jesus: "You are the Christ, the Son of the living God." This profession of faith pleased Jesus and with these words Jesus promised to give Peter authority to rule over his Church:

And I tell you, you are Peter, and on this rock I will build my church, and the powers of death shall not prevail against it. I will give you the keys of the kingdom of heaven, and whatever you bind on earth shall be bound in heaven, and whatever you loose on earth shall be loosed in heaven.   **Matthew 16:15-20**

Since the day of his Ascension was drawing near, Jesus wanted to appoint Peter to be the head of his Church, and to confer the primacy on him as he had promised. However, Jesus wanted Peter to accept this supreme office not simply as a command to be obeyed, not as an obligation thrust upon him. He wanted Peter to accept this challenge willingly, not out of a sense of duty, but out of love. To ascertain Peter's motivation, Jesus asked him, "Do you love me?" After each of Peter's professions of love, Jesus conferred the primacy upon Peter (see John 21:15ff):

"Feed my lambs."
"Tend my sheep."
"Feed my sheep."

But why did Jesus ask three times for an expression of Peter's love? Some maintain that since Peter had denied Jesus three times, Jesus wanted a triple profession of love. On the other hand, it may have been because of the gravity of the commission Peter was asked to undertake. Peter had to be motivated by love if he was to persevere in his mission. Each time Jesus requests us to undertake a special task, carry a burden, bear some pain, he first asks us, "Do you love me?" A Bantu proverb reminds us, "Love makes a burden light like a cloud."

LOVE IN ACTION

In these days of renewal and transition, the Church is striving to wean us away from the attitude of responding to the Lord merely out of a sense of duty or obligation. Instead we are called to fulfill the Lord's will as an expression of our love for him, to please him who loves us so much. This requires some appraisal of the reasons that motivate our actions.

Motivated by "law." Some of us harbor a legalistic approach in living our Christian way of life. We carefully try to observe all the laws, rules and regulations proposed by the Church and the Lord. While some faithfully keep these precepts, their dominant reason for obedience may be primarily fear of punishment if they fall short. Such people are motivated not by love for Jesus but by a sense of obligation.

Motivated by "love." We must strive to place more emphasis on love as the motivating incentive. Our love for the Lord should be our principal motivation in all that we do. If we truly love the Lord, we will make every effort to please him by fulfilling, to the best of our ability, all that he asks of us.

Love never counts the cost, nor does it tarry in doing whatever the Lord may ask. This is why Jesus asks us, "Do you love me?" Jesus makes it clear that we must love him in order to heed his Word and observe his directives. "He who has my commandments and keeps them, he it is who loves me.... If a man loves me, he will keep my word, and my Father will love him, and we will come to him and make our home with him" (Jn 14:21, 23).

In making the transition from a sense of duty and obligation to a loving response to the Lord, we must focus on our understanding of God. At times we may be tempted to think of God only in intellectual terms. This rational, theological attempt to know more about God and understand him with our minds is essential, but knowledge alone does not have the motivating power which is inherent in love.

A second approach to God is one currently being emphasized in the ongoing renewal of the Church. It is the heart approach, not simply knowing about God but knowing him. We long to know God as our personal, loving Father—a Father who created us, provides for us, loves us and forgives us when we fail him.

We want to know Jesus as a loving, personal God who loves us so much that he did not hesitate to lay down his life to redeem us. He loves us so much that he never leaves us but lives with us and within us in his resurrected, exalted life. This heart knowledge is called *appreciative knowledge,* while the theological knowledge is known as *cognitive knowledge.*

Knowing the Lord with our heart is vital to our spiritual growth and maturation. It is a necessary condition for love: We cannot love a person we do not know. Unless we know God as a loving, kind, gracious Lord, we cannot love him.

We come to know a person primarily by what that person reveals about himself or herself. Speech is self-revealing; it acquaints us with the person's attitude and disposition, likes and dislikes. The same is true of the Lord. We cannot know him with a cognitive knowledge, much less with an appreciative knowledge, unless we have at least a passing acquaintance with Scripture.

St. Jerome reminds us that ignorance of Scripture is ignorance of Christ. God's Word gives us insights into himself as a loving Person, and also helps us understand his will, mind and heart.

When we feel drawn to use Scripture as the basis of our prayer, we can use any or all of the principal methods of prayer. Some like to pray aloud, alone or with others. We can do so spontaneously or by using the words of Scripture, such as the Our Father or Mary's canticle of praise, the Magnificat. This is called vocal prayer.

Meditation is another method of praying with Scripture. It is a thought process reflecting on words of Scripture in order to reach a better understanding and appreciation of what the Lord is saying to us, and also to draw conclusions or guidelines for our daily living. When we reflect on the directive of Jesus to "love your neighbor as yourself," we can make a survey of our life and resolve to improve a strained relationship with another person.

A third method of praying with Scripture is a quiet listening with our heart to what Jesus is revealing about himself, either verbally or by his actions and attitudes. This method of prayer has various titles: wordless prayer, prayer of the heart, prayer of listening—all come under the umbrella of contemplation. The Holy Spirit is drawing more and more people into this method of prayer by giving them a longing and desire to know the Lord more intimately.

People in great numbers are taking time each day to rest and relax quietly with the Lord and to be inspired, motivated and guided by his Word in Scripture. We would do well to remember that even when we do not feel his love, our willingness to do whatever he wills is proof of our love for him. When Jesus asks us, "Do you love me?" may our response be as emphatic as Peter's: "Lord, you know everything; you know that I love you" (Jn 21:17).

For Reflection

One way we can determine how much we love the Lord is by taking time to ask ourselves various questions. The following questions are only suggestions; you may find it helpful to formulate your own.

- Do I try to keep myself aware that I am never alone, that Jesus is always abiding with me and within me?

- Do I hesitate to respond when I am asked to do a certain task not to my liking?

- Am I reluctant to accept some duty, pain, suffering or cross?

- Do I recognize and love Jesus dwelling in all the people I meet?

- Do I pause to listen when the Lord asks, "Do you love me?" How do I respond?

CHAPTER SEVEN

"What Do You Want Me to Do for You?"

WHEN WE USE SCRIPTURE as the basis of our prayer, we must remember that the Lord himself is speaking to us. As the Second Vatican Council reminds us, "He (Christ) is present in his Word, since it is he himself who speaks when the holy scriptures are read in the Church."[1] We must, therefore, be receptive to what he is saying to us. Our attitude should be, "Lord, what are you saying to me?"

In the Gospel, Jesus poses two soul-searching questions to us as he did to the blind men: "What do you want me to do for you?" and "Do you believe I am able to do this?"

JESUS AND BLIND BARTIMAEUS

When Jesus was on his way to Jerusalem for the Passover Feast, he met blind Bartimaeus on the roadside near Jericho. To orient ourselves and also to appreciate all the nuances involved in this event, we should read and reflect on the scene related in the Gospel, concentrating on the person of Bartimaeus. Move slowly through the whole event with a listening heart and an open mind. We may come to realize that we, too, may be spiritually blind and desire to see more vividly.

And they came to Jericho; and as he was leaving Jericho with his disciples and a great multitude, Bartimaeus, a blind beggar, the son of Timaeus, was sitting by the roadside. And when he heard that it was Jesus of Nazareth, he began to cry out and say, "Jesus, Son of David, have mercy on me!" ... And Jesus stopped and said, "Call him." And they called the blind man; saying to him, "Take heart; rise, he is calling you." And throwing off his mantle he sprang up and came to Jesus. And Jesus said to him, "What do you want me to do for you?" And the blind man said to him, "Master, let me receive my sight." And Jesus said to him, "Go your way; your faith has made you well." And immediately he received his sight and followed him on the way.

Mark 10:46-52

In those days the common means of travel was on foot. Since traveling was slow and tedious, people often walked with a rabbi, listening to his teaching as they journeyed along, much as walkers and joggers today use cassette players or radios with headphones. Jesus also used this peripatetic method of teaching. As they passed a village, people would walk a longer or shorter distance to catch up on the latest news or to listen to some teaching. On this occasion, many of Jesus' listeners were also going to Jerusalem for the Passover.

Some aspects of this event, especially the role of Bartimaeus, may speak to us about our own attitudes. The sheer persistence of Bartimaeus crying out to Jesus may encourage us to examine our prayer of petition. Do we ask only once before deciding that the Lord will not grant our request? At times the Lord wants us to continue to seek his help. Our repeated queries purify our own intentions and clearly demonstrate our humble dependence on God and our trust and confidence in him. Just as Bartimaeus would not be put off even though the crowd tried to silence him, we, too, should not become discouraged if our request is not answered immediately, but should continue to implore the Lord's help.

DISCARD ALL HINDRANCES

When Jesus called Bartimaeus to come to him, immediately and without hesitation he threw aside his cloak, lest it would impede him from reaching Jesus as soon as possible. Recall that a cloak was a very important item of clothing, especially for a beggar. It kept him warm and served as a begging cushion by day and as a bed at night. If Bartimaeus were not healed, it would be difficult for the blind man to find his cloak in this huge crowd following Jesus.

When Jesus invites us to assume some special undertaking, are we impeded by our "cloak"? Is there anything in our lives that causes us to hesitate in responding to the inspirations of his grace, or hinders us in deepening our personal relationship with Jesus? Are we so preoccupied with some mundane program or project that we do not hear the Lord inviting us? Are we usually too busy and in too great a hurry to "waste time" with the Lord? Are we hampered by a "cloak" of fatigue, too tired and overworked from striving to meet the expectations of others? Jesus knew that this could happen to us, and that is why he invites us: "Come to me all who labor and are heavy laden, and I will give you rest" (Mt 11:28). He also reminds us, "Apart from me you can do nothing" (Jn 15:5).

"MASTER, LET ME RECEIVE MY SIGHT."

When Bartimaeus reached Jesus, he knew precisely what he wanted: "Master, let me receive my sight." When we approach the Lord, we should likewise know exactly the special grace we need or the kind of help we are seeking. This may require some honest, sincere discernment or an objective self-examination to determine whether our request is conducive to our growth in holiness or if it merely satisfies a selfish desire.

Jesus knows all about our humanness and our self-centeredness; hence he asks us, "What do you want me to do for you?" May our fervent plea be the same as Bartimaeus' request: "Master, let me receive my sight." Perhaps we want to see more clearly whatever there is in our life that is preventing us from being open and responsive to the Lord's plan for us. We may want to see so that we might recognize the Lord's will in all the happenings of the day. We may want to see more clearly the Lord's abiding presence in every person we meet. May our daily prayer be "Master, let me receive my sight."

Bartimaeus' faith, confidence and trust in the loving concern and kindness of Jesus was quite evident. He believed in the power of Jesus to heal, and Jesus' response indicates that this pleased him very much: "Go your way; your faith has made you well."

How frequently in the Gospels Jesus reminds us that faith in him motivated him to use his divine power to heal and forgive. On the other hand, Matthew tells us that when Jesus returned to Nazareth, the people did not believe in him. How pathetic are the words of the Gospel: "He did not do many mighty works there, because of their unbelief" (Mt 13:58).

LOOKING WITH EYES OF FAITH

Jesus did not just restore Bartimaeus' physical sight; he gave the formerly blind man a much deeper spiritual vision. He rewarded the faith of Bartimaeus by bestowing on him an instantaneous understanding of discipleship. With his sudden and profound insight, Bartimaeus made his commitment to Jesus and "followed him down the road." It is evident in the original text that "the road" is the way of discipleship to which Jesus called him. Without hesitation Bartimaeus followed him.

It may require considerable prayer, soul-searching and discernment to clarify and formulate our response to Jesus when he asks us, "What do you want me to do for you?"

JESUS HEALS TWO BLIND MEN

Blindness was a common malady in the Near East at the time of Jesus, and still is today. It is caused by many factors: the unprotected glare of the eastern sun, infections caused by a lack of cleanliness, or the cloud of flies that usually hover about. Jesus frequently healed the blind men and women who were brought to him. The Gospel of Matthew records one such occasion when Jesus encountered two blind men in a crowd:

> And as Jesus passed on from there, two blind men followed him, crying aloud, "Have mercy on us, Son of David." When he entered the house, the blind men came to him....   **Matthew 9:27-28**

This passage may startle some people when they discover that Jesus did not heal these two men on the spot! There may have been several reasons that Jesus did not respond immediately to their request. In the first place, the blind men called him the "Son of David," which was a popular messianic concept at that time, referring to one who would free them all from the domination of Rome and restore their nation to power and greatness. The blind men may have regarded Jesus as a wonder-worker who would lead their people to freedom and conquest.

Secondly, Jesus may have wanted the blind men to be aware that a healing would mean a change in their lifestyle. If they were healed they would have to assume responsibility for earning their own living. Only handicapped persons were permitted to beg for a living. Jesus wanted to make sure that they understood and were sincere in asking to have their sight restored.

It may be that Jesus had wanted to elicit an expression of faith in him as the real Messiah. He may have wanted to test their faith away from the enthusiasm of the crowd, to make them aware that his healing power was divine. Once they were in the house, he asked them a direct question to ascertain the level of their faith:

> And Jesus said to them, "Do you believe that I am able to do this?" They said to him, "Yes, Lord." Then he touched their eyes, saying, "According to your faith be it done to you." And their eyes were opened.
>
> **Matthew 9:28-29**

ALONE WITH GOD WE FIND HEALING

It is interesting to note that Jesus wanted to deal with these blind men alone. He did not respond to their request out on the street. While they were with the crowd, they could be carried away with the enthusiasm and shouting of the people as Jesus passed by. Only when they were alone could they be sincere in begging for this healing.

When we approach Jesus with a special request, he may not respond immediately nor grant the precise favor we are asking. Jesus is anxious to confer with us alone, as he did with the two blind men. Alone with him in prayer, we can more easily discover if our petition is too self-centered or too vague, and whether we have a deep understanding of its implications. Repeating our request again and again will manifest our dependence upon him, purify our intentions, and also make us more appreciative of the Lord's bountiful goodness to us.

Lest we begin to doubt his providential love, or are inclined to waver in imploring his help, Jesus asks us, "Do you believe that I am able to do this?" In other words, he is asking us to examine our own faith in his loving concern for us. It pleases the Lord very much when we walk daily and hourly with an expectant faith, realizing that he loves us so much that he cares for us at every moment of the day, even in the slightest things in life. Recognizing his boundless love elicits a loving response from us.

CONFIDENCE AND TRUST IN GOD

Confidence and trust are the fruits of love. We place all our trust and confidence in the person we love. When we genuinely love the Lord, we are willing to say our YES to him, confident that he wills only what is for our good.

Confidence in God and confidence in ourselves are closely connected and can be confused. Sometimes when we say that we have lost confidence and trust in God, we really mean that we have lost confidence in ourselves. When we think we have no self-confidence, we have really lost our confidence in the Lord's loving care and concern for us. When all is going well in life, we usually have boundless confidence in ourselves, but perhaps our thoughts of God are rather remote. However, when trials, difficulties and hardships arise, we lose confidence in managing our own affairs and turn to the Lord, hoping he will come to our rescue.

A certain man was anxiously leaning over the rail at a racetrack, begging and pleading with the Lord to permit his horse to come in first and earn him some much-needed money. He had bet his last few dollars on a horse, disregarding the dire needs of his family. As he prayed, his horse took a commanding lead. As the horse came down the homestretch, it was quite apparent that no other horse could overtake him. At this point the man shouted, "Never mind, God, I can take it from here."

In our society such an attitude is prevalent. We are influenced by the atmosphere of secularism and materialism surrounding us; in this climate we can become self-sufficient as we try to prove our self-worth. However, this kind of self-confidence, spawned by pride, begins to wane when we fail in our efforts to meet the standards others expect of us. We are like the little boy who refuses his parents' help with "I can do it myself." These failures awaken us to the Lord's caution that without him we can do nothing. When the Lord comes to our rescue and picks us up when we fail, our confidence in him and our confidence in ourselves begin to build again.

MARY, OUR MODEL

At the wedding feast in Cana, Mary, our Mother, manifested her total trust and confidence in her Son. Jesus did not seem to be concerned about his Mother's observation, "They have no wine." Mary was not daunted by Jesus' initial negative response. She trusted that her Son would respond because of his loving care and compassion. Her confidence prompted her to advise the attendants, "Do whatever he tells you" (Jn 2:1ff). The attendants filled the water pots, enabling him to work the first miracle of his public ministry.

Daily Jesus asks us, "What do you want me to do for you?" and "Do you believe that I am able to do this?"

❦

For Reflection

That we may grow and mature on our journey heavenward, it is essential for us to take some quiet time to sit with the Lord in order to ascertain the depths of our faith, love and trust in him.

- Is my confidence and trust in the Lord constant and unwavering regardless of what might arise in the course of the day?

- How often do I ask the Lord to remove my spiritual blindness, that I may always find and fulfill his will in all the happenings of life?

- Do I easily become discouraged and disturbed when my prayers are not answered at the time and in the way I have asked?

- In the stories of Bartimaeus and the two blind men, what impressed me most? Did I glean any resolve or motivation from these scriptural accounts?

CHAPTER EIGHT

"Before Abraham Was, I Am."

IN THE PREVIOUS CHAPTER, we accompanied Jesus in spirit as he used his divine power to heal blind Bartimaeus and two other blind men who had followed Jesus, begging him to restore their sight. These two men heard the crowd proclaiming Jesus as the Son of David, but they may not have realized that he was God. To test their faith, Jesus asked them if they were confident that he had the power to heal them. In the Gospel, Jesus clearly revealed his identity as God when he claimed the title "I AM" for himself.

Wherever Jesus went, teaching and healing, the Jewish leaders dogged his footsteps. They challenged his authority and his right to teach since he was not educated in the rabbinical schools. They could not deny his miracles so they attributed his power to the devil working in him. They demanded to know his real identity.

When they insisted on knowing his origin and identity, Jesus replied, "You are from below, I am from above; you are of this world, I am not of this world.... When you have lifted up the Son of man, then you will know that I am he...." (Jn 8:23, 28). In doing so, Jesus was clearly proclaiming his divinity; this was the name by which God identified himself from the very dawn of history. The religious leaders certainly understood that he was proclaiming himself to be God, but, lacking faith, they refused to accept his claim. As the Jews continued to challenge him, Jesus informed them that he had existed from all eternity when he solemnly declared, "Truly, truly, I say to you, before Abraham was, I am" (Jn 8:58).

HOW DID JESUS' CONTEMPORARIES RESPOND?

When Jesus called himself "I AM," he was using the name by which the Jews had known God throughout their history. When God called to Moses from the burning bush and directed him to go to Egypt to free his enslaved people, Moses asked the Lord, "Who shall I say sent me?" God replied, "I AM WHO I AM." Then God added, "Say this to the people of Israel, 'I AM has sent me to you'" (Ex 3:13ff).

This utterance "I AM WHO I AM" is the origin of the word Yahweh, which the Jews used as the proper and personal name of God. Out of reverence and awe, they did not address the Lord as "I AM," but as "Yahweh."

On Mt. Horeb, when Moses received the two stone tablets of the Law, I AM revealed more about himself and his divine attributes. "The Lord, the Lord, a God merciful and gracious, slow to anger and abounding in steadfast love and faithfulness" (Ex 34:6). Jesus revealed himself to his contemporaries as this very God in whom they believed, the one they worshiped.

The problem for the Jewish leaders was not a lack of evidence of Christ's divinity. It was their lack of humility and faith that prevented them from believing in Jesus and accepting him as the promised Messiah. Throughout his public ministry, Jesus pleaded for faith in himself and in his teachings. He was pleased when someone expressed faith in him, and disappointed when such faith was missing. How often Jesus said to a person seeking healing or forgiveness, "Your faith has saved you."

When Jesus gave up his life on the cross for the redemption of mankind, a spark of faith was ignited in the heart of a Roman centurion. Before the gloating crowd of the enemies of Jesus, the centurion openly professed his faith in Jesus. Witnessing the death of Jesus, the centurion said, "Truly, this man was the Son of God" (Mk 15:39). By his profession of faith, the centurion verified the prophecy of Jesus, "When you have lifted up the Son of man, then you will know that I am he" (Jn 8:28).

CRISIS OF FAITH IN TODAY'S SOCIETY

Since that day on the hill of Calvary, countless men and women have contemplated the love that prompted the passion and death of Jesus, and have experienced a rekindling of faith, a more fervent love, and a deeper commitment to the Lord. This fulfills another prophecy of Jesus: "And I, when I am lifted up from the earth, will draw all men to myself" (Jn 12:32).

In our society today there is a devastating crisis in faith. The primary cause of so much of the injustice, violence, greed and human rights violations is a woeful lack of faith in God and in others. Many no longer walk with the Lord because their eroded faith cannot accept his way of life. Some do not accompany him because they do not know him and the great love he has for them. Some even doubt that he is God, the I AM.

There are many reasons for this crisis in faith. High on the list is the widespread ignorance about the Lord, his Church, and what we are called to be and to do. Many people are only partially catechized with little or no updating of their faith since elementary or high school days (other than attending Sunday Mass). These people live on what they have learned in their early years, neglecting their adult education. For the most part, the educational or formational level of the Christian community leaves much to be desired.

Extraordinary advances in technology have made us a very proud, sophisticated people who feel little or no need for God. In our self-sufficiency, some have determined their own moral code of conduct, which often conflicts with the standard the Lord himself set up for us. Self-centeredness and greed have led many people down a path away from the laws of God, especially his law of love.

In the present crisis of faith, of unrest and uncertainty, the Lord calls each of us to become a beacon, a paragon of faith, in the midst of a confused, materialistic society. Our lifestyle can have a powerful influence on an untold number of people, without our even being aware of it. In all the events of the day, our attitudes and actions will reflect a life of committed faith in all the ups and downs of life. A vibrant, expectant faith enables us to rely totally on the Lord, knowing that his providential love overshadows us unfailingly. A cheerful confidence and trust in our heavenly Father's loving care and concern shines through us and produces a peace and joy within our hearts that radiates in all our undertakings.

Even our faltering attempts at faith are rewarded and strengthened by God's grace. When a father asked Jesus to heal his son possessed by a demon, Jesus replied, "All things are possible to him who believes." Then the boy's father cried out, "I believe; help my unbelief" (Mk 9:23ff). The whole crowd was utterly amazed and began to realize that the father's faith and confidence in the Lord's healing power enabled Jesus to heal this man's son. This event afforded Jesus another opportunity to prove that he is "I AM."

Jesus himself calls us to be his disciples and to radiate a dynamic, expectant faith in him. As Jesus himself said, "You are the light of the world.... Let your light so shine before men, that they may see your good works and give glory to your Father who is in heaven" (Mt 5:14ff).

COMMISSIONED TO REACH OUT

The Lord calls and commissions us to "go and make disciples of all nations" by giving witness to our faith in him and by our Christian love for others. If we are to be staunch pillars of expectant faith and the personification of Christlike love in our environment, our own faith must be vibrant, dynamic and operative; our love for others must be constant and sincere.

Our own faith and love will depend on how well we know the Lord with a heart knowledge, rather than only a cognitive or intellectual knowledge. We must recognize him as a personal God who loves us, cares for us, forgives us, heals us and meets all of our needs. In order to be convinced of this, we must listen with our whole being to what he is telling us about himself.

Prayerfully listening to our I AM speaking to us in our hearts will deepen our love and appreciation, our awe and reverence, and will at the same time enable us to assess the depths of our own relationship to him. Recalling the blessings of the Father, Son and Holy Spirit will enable us to grow and mature in our love for him and equip us to become faithful witnesses of his tender loving care and concern for all his creatures.

Each of the three members of the Trinity reflect a different aspect of God's concern and character. Let us explore how each divine Person uniquely expresses God's loving and compassionate care for us:

THE FATHER IS "I AM"...

...who is the transcendent God of heaven and earth, the God of majesty and glory, of might and power, whom the host of heaven adore, praise and magnify unceasingly. "Holy, holy, holy is the Lord God Almighty, who was and is and is to come" (Rv 4:8).

...who created us in his own image and likeness because he loves us. "I made the earth and created man upon it" (Is 45:12).

...who adopts us as his children, giving us our privileged dignity as he welcomes us into the family of God. "I will live in them and move among them, and I will be their God and they shall be my people" (2 Cor 6:16).

...who loves us with an infinite, unconditional, unchanging love, regardless of who we are, or what we have done or not done. "Because you are precious in my eyes, and honored, and I love you" (Is 43:4).

...whose providential caring and concerned love provides all our needs. He asks, "What more was there to do for my vineyard, that I have not done in it?" (Is 5:4).

...whose compassionate, merciful, forgiving love is always eager to pardon and forgive us when we sin. "My steadfast love shall not depart from you, and my covenant of peace shall not be removed, says the Lord, who has compassion on you" (Is 54:10).

...who heals us physically, emotionally and spiritually when we implore his healing love. "I am the Lord, your healer" (Ex 15:26).

...who loves us so much that "he gave us his only Son, that whoever believes in him should not perish but have eternal life" (Jn 3:16).

JESUS IS OUR "I AM"...

...who reveals his boundless love for us when he explains, "As the Father has loved me, so have I loved you" (Jn 15:9). He also assures us of the intensity of his love: "Greater love has no man than this, that a man lay down his life for his friends" (Jn 15:13).

...who could not leave us orphans but promised to be with us, to journey with us through all the happenings in our life and take us by the hand when we are uncertain, bewildered or fearful. "Lo, I am with you always, to the close of the age" (Mt 28:20).

...who is always eager to forgive us when we sin, provided we humbly and contritely seek his mercy and pardon. We can be certain that his oft-spoken words will linger in our hearts: "My son, your sins are forgiven" (Mk 2:5).

...who comforts, consoles and heals our wounded hearts when we are hurt, insulted, discouraged, angry, resentful or disappointed. Jesus says, "Let not your hearts be troubled; believe in God, believe also in me" (Jn 14:1).

...whose resurrection from the dead confirms our own rising to be united with him in the eternal bliss of heaven. He gave us his promise: "I am the resurrection and the life; he who believes in me, though he die, yet shall he live" (Jn 11:25), and "I will come back again and take you to myself, that where I am you may be also" (Jn 14:3).

THE HOLY SPIRIT IS THE "I AM"...

...whose special role, as the third Person of the Blessed Trinity, is to be our Sanctifier. By his abiding presence and divine power he leads and transforms us on our journey heavenward.

...who made us his temple, living within us to inspire, enlighten, encourage and motivate us in our pursuit of the eternal joy of heaven. Paul asks, "Do you not know that you are God's temple and that God's Spirit dwells in you?" (1 Cor 3:16).

...who is the source of divine love empowering us to love God with all our heart, to love ourselves just as we are and to love our neighbor as ourselves. "God's love has been poured into our hearts through the Holy Spirit which has been given to us" (Rom 5:5).

...who implants the seed of faith in our hearts and by his divine influence helps us to nurture and strengthen that seed as it develops from an intellectual faith into a faith of commitment, and finally into a faith of expectancy. "No one can say 'Jesus is Lord' except by the Holy Spirit" (1 Cor 12:3).

...who teaches us how to pray as he penetrates our human ego to give us insights beyond our human comprehension. "Likewise the Spirit helps us in our weakness; for we do not know how to pray as we ought, but the Spirit himself intercedes for us with sighs too deep for words" (Rom 8:26).

...who is our Comforter, bestowing his gifts upon us so that we may reflect his love in our attitudes and actions toward family, friends, and all those the Lord sends our way. "The fruit of the Spirit is love, joy, peace, patience, kindness, goodness, faithfulness, gentleness, self-control" (Gal 5:22).

...who heals our spiritual blindness by granting us a genuine spirit of discernment, enabling us to distinguish the movements within us to determine whether they are coming from God or from the evil one. "To each is given the manifestation of the Spirit for the common good. To one is given through the Spirit... the ability to distinguish between spirits" (1 Cor 12:7ff).

...who protects and strengthens us in times of trial and temptation, that we may not succumb but be encouraged by the example of Jesus, especially as he dealt with the temptations in the desert. "But the Lord is faithful; he will strengthen you and guard you from evil" (2 Thes 3:3).

As we grow in our knowledge and appreciation of the Lord as our all-powerful, majestic and loving I AM, we will be better prepared to respond to his questions, if he should ask us as he did the blind men, "What do you want me to do for you?" or "Do you believe that I am able to do this?"

❦

For Reflection

Take a moment to reflect on your relationship with the Father, the Son and the Holy Spirit:

• Do I daily praise and thank my Father for my existence and for his love and blessings that sustain me and fulfill all my spiritual and temporal needs?

- Does my appreciation of the redeeming love of Jesus manifest itself by my earnestly striving to live his way of life and to love him in return?

- How often do I reflect on the abiding presence of the Holy Spirit, the Sanctifier, within me to inspire and guide, to strengthen and encourage me and above all to fill me with his love as I tread the pathway of life?

- At the close of the day do I take time to thank the Lord for three or four special gifts I have received that day? Does my spirit of joyous gratitude encourage others to thank God for his bounteous gifts and blessings?

CHAPTER NINE

"Who Is My Mother?"

ACCORDING TO HIS ETERNAL PLAN, God created and designated the family as the basic unit of society. Originating in a common blood relationship, and united and strengthened by bonds of love, the family is a closely knit community. In the ideal family, as intended by God, the children have a sense of gratitude and respect for their parents. The Lord stated this condition as one of the Ten Commandments: "Honor your father and mother" (Ex 20:12).

In a family we find a unique loyalty and great care and concern for one another. A good Christian family is a haven in which love and understanding, comfort and relaxation, support and encouragement abound. According to God's design it is in the family setting that we first learn to love one another. It is also in our home where we come to know that God loves us, and where we in turn learn to love him. How grateful we are for God's providential plan to supply all our needs as we journey through life.

LESSONS FROM THE HOLY FAMILY

In the little home at Nazareth, Jesus, Mary and Joseph lived a perfect family life, since they were united in mutual bonds of love, reverence and respect. With Jesus in their midst, it was surely the vestibule of heaven. However, Scripture relates an incident during the public ministry of Jesus that, at first reading, may cause us to wonder if perhaps Jesus' filial love for his mother was beginning to wane as he traversed the highways and byways, announcing the good news of his kingdom to those who would listen. As we recall this incident in the Gospel, we may be puzzled at the response of Jesus.

> While he was still speaking to the people, behold, his mother and his brothers stood outside, asking to speak to him. But he replied to the man who told him, "Who is my mother, and who are my brothers?" And stretching out his hand toward his disciples, he said, "Here are my mother and my brothers! For whoever does the will of my Father in heaven is my brother, and sister, and mother."
>
> **Matthew 12:46-50**

At first we may be startled by Jesus' question: "Who is my mother? Who are my brothers and my sisters?" In no way did Jesus intend to minimize the importance of the human family or the relationship that the members should have with one another. Least of all did he intend to infer any lack of appreciation for Mary's important role in his life or any ebbing of his infinite love for her. The love which Jesus has for every human being is unconditional and unchanging, which assures us that his love for his mother would never change. Surely Mary was loved by her Divine Son as no other mother was loved by a son.

Jesus used this occasion to point out to his disciples and to us that there are two distinct familial relationships, the human family and the spiritual family, which are by no means mutually exclusive but rather complementary.

FACETS OF THE HUMAN FAMILY

In his providential plan for mankind, the Father intended the human family to be a closely knit unit of society to provide and care for the temporal welfare of all its members. Love must bind all the members into a community of peace and harmony. Together the family grows and matures in their pursuit of holiness, education, business and social life. The family setting is a kind of prep school instructing, preparing and conditioning us for our role in life. Enriched by God's special gift of love, the family grows in understanding and encouragement, in appreciation and loyalty to one another.

Our "natural" family. One of the brief but troublesome directives Jesus gave us makes the home the ideal place to put his will into practice: "You shall love your neighbor as yourself" (Mt 22:39). Created in the image and likeness of God who is love, every human being longs to love and be loved. The family unit is the first and foremost setting to implement the Lord's directive. Here we experience being loved and appreciated. It also gives us every opportunity to reach out in loving concern for all the members of the family.

In the Holy Family's home in Nazareth, all the components for the ideal family were present and practiced to an eminent degree. Jesus deeply appreciated his human family, especially the role his mother fulfilled so perfectly during his sojourn on earth.

Our spiritual family. As Christians we have a unique privilege of enjoying a dual family membership. We are born into our natural or human family, and by baptism we are incorporated into the family of God as he adopts us as his sons and daughters. This is our spiritual family. One of the extraordinary fruits of baptism is the coming of the Lord to dwell with us and within us, sharing his divine life and love to the extent that we have the capacity to receive it.

Jesus teaches us this profound truth when he tells us "If a man loves me, he will keep my word, and my Father will love him, and we will come to him and make our home with him" (Jn 14:23). The dwelling of which Jesus speaks is his permanent, abiding presence with us. St. Paul reminds us of this teaching of Jesus as the fruit of baptism. He asks: "Do you not know that you are God's temple and that God's Spirit dwells in you?" (1 Cor 3:16).

As the source of divine love, the Holy Spirit fills us with his love, enabling us to recognize the will of God in every situation we encounter in life. He enlightens us to discern God's will and strengthens us to do whatever the Lord asks of us. The Spirit reminds us of the words of Jesus: "Without me you can do nothing." With these words he implies that with him we can do all things.

Our spiritual family has some very broad dimensions. It embraces the whole host of heaven, all the angels and saints who intercede for us all the days of our lives. Mary the Mother of Jesus, Queen of the angels and saints, and our Mother also, is deeply concerned about our spiritual and temporal welfare. By her powerful intercession she obtains for us all the gifts and graces we need as we journey along the highway of life.

Dual "family membership." Dual membership in our human and spiritual families is of paramount importance for our life here and in the hereafter. During our earthly sojourn this twofold membership is essential for our physical and spiritual welfare. However, our spiritual family takes precedence, since it endures for all eternity, while our human family is temporal. This is the lesson Jesus taught when he asked, "Who is my mother? Who are my brothers and sisters?" His mother's spiritual relationship to him was more important, for her sake, than her being the mother of his humanity.

WHO IS IN JESUS' SPIRITUAL FAMILY?

Jesus does not say in Scripture that everyone who simply hears his word—or who seeks him out for an ulterior reason—will be a member of his spiritual family. This role belongs only to those who choose to become his disciples. Jesus made a distinction between a follower and a disciple. A disciple does not merely walk in the footsteps of the Master but follows him so closely that he can be identified with him. A person who strives to put on the mind and heart of Jesus, who is eager to fulfill his will and live his way of life, will be Jesus' disciple. Jesus made it clear that only disciples were members of his spiritual family—the family of God:

> And stretching out his hand toward his disciples, he said, "Here are my mother and my brothers! For whoever does the will of my Father in heaven is my brother, and sister, and mother." **Matthew 12:49-50**

Jesus used this occasion to correct a false notion that was prevalent among the Jews of his day. They believed that, since they were of the lineage of Abraham, they were the chosen people of God and would automatically reach their heavenly reward. In this passage, Jesus attempted to convince the Jewish leaders that spiritual adoption into the family of God was far more important than being able to trace one's natural genealogy back to Abraham's family. Yet they contended, "We are descendants of Abraham, and have never been in bondage to any one" (Jn 8:33). Thus they exonerated themselves from accepting Jesus and his teachings.

MARY: THE FIRST AND PERFECT DISCIPLE

Obviously Mary is not merely a follower of Jesus but his very first disciple. Mary is the first and most perfect disciple of Jesus. Throughout Mary's earliest years, the Holy Spirit enlightened, strengthened and transformed her, enabling her to keep her mind and heart perfectly in tune with the Father's plan for her in the economy of salvation.

Motivated by her overwhelming love, Mary became the first disciple to follow the way of life that Jesus was teaching. She lived by his word. When a woman in the crowd praised Mary for being his mother, Jesus himself attested to the real reason for her blessedness: "Blessed rather are those who hear the word of God and keep it!" (Lk 11:28). Mary heard the word of God and put it into practice in her life.

Mary and the early ministry of Jesus. At the very outset of the public ministry of Jesus, Mary proved herself to be a solicitous mother as well as a faithful disciple. One example is found in the second chapter of the Gospel of John:

> There was a marriage at Cana in Galilee, and the mother of Jesus was there; Jesus also was invited to the marriage, with his disciples. When the wine gave out, the mother of Jesus said to him, "They have no wine." And Jesus said to her, "O woman, what have you to do with me? My hour has not yet come." His mother said to the servants, "Do whatever he tells you." **John 2:1-5**

When Jesus asked the servers to fill the six stone jars, each holding twenty to thirty gallons, with water, they obeyed—even though it was a difficult task because the water had to be carried in small amounts from the spring. Because the servers cooperated, Jesus was able to supply sufficient wine for the celebration by working his first miracle at the request of his mother. The poet Richard

Crashaw's description is more picturesque: "The modest water saw its God and blushed."[1] Although we don't know the reason why Jesus chose to perform this miracle at this time, we may surmise that Jesus was anxious to reveal the power of Mary's prayerful intercession.

Mary and the early church. After the Ascension of Jesus into heaven, the apostles and "about one hundred and twenty persons" gathered in the Upper Room to wait for the coming of the Holy Spirit, as the Father had promised. "All these with one accord devoted themselves to prayer, together with the women and Mary the mother of Jesus, and with his brothers" (Acts 1:14).

True to her calling, Mary prayed fervently for the outpouring of the Holy Spirit upon the apostles, who were commissioned by Jesus to go and "make disciples of all nations... teaching them to observe all that I commanded you" (Mt 28:19). The *Catechism of the Catholic Church* (hereafter, "the *Catechism*") teaches that Mary "aided the beginnings of the church by her prayers... by her prayers [she implored] the gift of the Spirit, who had already overshadowed her in the Annunciation" (#965). As she was present to the Church in those early days, she is likewise present to us, since we are the Church today.

Mary: Mother of the Church today. On Calvary, Jesus gave us his mother to be our spiritual Mother in the order of grace. Her gracious maternal concern to love, intercede and care for all her spiritual children will continue for all time. The *Catechism* states it in these words (#969):

> This motherhood of Mary in the order of grace continues uninterruptedly from the consent which she loyally gave at the Annunciation and which she sustained without wavering beneath the cross, until the eternal

fulfillment of all the elect. Taken up to heaven she did not lay aside this saving office but by her manifold intercession continues to bring us the gifts of eternal salvation.

Mary proved her true Motherhood at Cana and again in the Upper Room. A mother is always eager to serve others, especially her loved ones. She encourages them in their worries and rejoices in their happiness.

Mary was always conscious of her Son's mission and aware of his power and his eagerness to come to the aid of anyone who humbly implored him with faith. As our spiritual Mother, Mary's mission continues in our lives today. She is deeply concerned about both our spiritual welfare and our earthly well-being. She realizes that the manifold blessings of God will be showered upon us if we strive to discern and fulfill his will in all the happenings of the day. Her admonition remains always the same: "Do whatever he tells you."

In striving to do so, we will be Jesus' disciples and credible members of the household of God: "For whoever does the will of my Father in heaven is my brother, and sister, and mother" (Mt 12:50).

For Reflection

Just as a family must pause occasionally to reassess its direction, we, too, will find it profitable to examine our own attitudes and to appreciate our privileged membership in the spiritual family of God.

- Do I keep myself aware of my dignity and responsibility as a member of my spiritual family, with God as my loving Father, Jesus my compassionate Brother and Mary my solicitous Mother?

- As a disciple of Jesus, do I reflect his love, peace and joy to everyone I meet in my daily encounters?

- Do I ask Mary, my Mother, for her prayerful help that I may always be able to do whatever he tells me?

- Is Jesus happy to call me his brother or sister?

CHAPTER TEN

"I Am the True Vine."

IN THE PREVIOUS CHAPTER, Jesus explained how our spiritual relationship with him takes precedence over our relationship with our human family. In his own inimitable way, he now clarifies this teaching by relating the parable of the vine and branches.

As a teacher, Jesus had no equal. He often used parables to explain profound truths that his audience—and we today—might not otherwise have grasped. A parable is a story, an illustration or a figure of speech that explains a mystery or a spiritual truth in such a way that our finite minds might arrive at some understanding of it. Embodied in Jesus' parables we discover a wealth of information, applications, directives and reflections for our spiritual growth.

VINEYARD OF GOD

When Jesus introduced himself as the True Vine, his hearers already had some notion of the importance of the vine in Jewish history. The vine was a part of the religious heritage of the chosen people. In the Old Testament, the relationship of Israel to God is often portrayed as the vine or vineyard of the Lord.

Unfortunately, the symbolism was often negative: tvines typically produced wild grapes, signifying Israel's straying away from God. When the prophets speak of Israel as the "vine of God," it is almost always in the context of the nation's deplorable state of degeneration. The Lord frequently laments, "What more was there to do for my vineyard, that I have not done in it?" (Is 5:4).

There was also a belief among the Jews that their salvation was guaranteed simply by belonging to the nation of Israel, as a branch on the vine of God. Jesus emphatically dispelled this notion when he proclaimed that he was the True Vine (Jn 15:1), the only authentic vine. Faith in Jesus, the True Vine, establishes an intimate personal relationship with him, which enables us to become a productive branch by following his way of life.

BRANCHES OF THE TRUE VINE

In relating the parable of the vine and branches, Jesus revealed the unique and privileged relationship we enjoy with him as branches on the vine. It is inconceivable that any relationship could exist in a closer bond of unity and dependence than the bond in which Jesus reveals himself as the True Vine, and us as the branches.

As we ponder the words of Jesus in the parable of the vine and branches, we appreciate even more the mysterious bond of love that unites us to him. Each time we reflectively read his words, we enjoy new insights and challenges:

I am the true vine, and my Father is the vinedresser. Every branch of mine that bears no fruit, he takes away, and every branch that does bear fruit he prunes, that it may bear more fruit. You are already made clean by the word which I have spoken to you. Abide in me, and I in you. As the branch cannot bear fruit by itself, unless it abides in the vine, neither can you, unless you abide in me. I am the vine, you are the branches. He who abides in me, and I in him, he it is that bears much fruit, for apart from me you can do nothing. If a man does not abide in me, he is cast forth as a branch and withers; and the branches are gathered, thrown into the fire and burned. If you abide in me, and my words abide in you, ask whatever you will, and it shall be done for you. By this my Father is glorified, that you bear much fruit, and so prove to be my disciples. As the Father has loved me, so have I loved you; abide in my love. If you keep my commandments, you will abide in my love, just as I have kept my Father's commandments and abide in his love.

John 15:1-10

As we contemplate the mystery of the divine indwelling that is seen in the parable of the vine and branches, it baffles our imagination. While the words of Jesus are quite understandable, the mystery is too profound for our human minds. The transcendent God of heaven and earth, the Sustainer and Energizer of the whole universe, longs to abide within us to fill us with his divine life and love. His providential love has provided all the means necessary to establish this unique relationship with him.

Lest we become overwhelmed by this outpouring of the goodness of God, the Father calms our anxiety when he tells us: "Fear not, for I have redeemed you; I have called you by name, you are mine" (Is 43:1). Jesus, aware that we could not grasp all the implications of this mysterious union, revealed it to us in the parable of the vine and the branches in order to lead us to a deeper appreciation of this profound truth.

We are precious and privileged branches created by our loving Father, the Vine Dresser. A characteristic of love is its longing to give and share with the beloved. So immense is the Lord's love that he wants to share himself with us to the fullest extent our humanity is capable of receiving him. We first receive this love in the waters of baptism.

BAPTIZED INTO THE BODY OF CHRIST

Through baptism we are incorporated into Christ, just as a branch is grafted onto a life-giving vine. By his indwelling the Lord makes us Christians in a very real sense. St. Paul frequently speaks about this unique incorporation into Christ and the Lord's dynamic presence in us: "Do you not know that you are God's temple and that God's spirit dwells in you?" (1 Cor 3:16).

The Spirit does not rest within us in a static state, but is operative and dynamic within us, inspiring, motivating, enlightening and loving us. Jesus speaks of his presence within us as "living water" (Jn 7:38), an element absolutely essential to the preservation of life.

St. Paul also reminds us of our very special relationship with the Lord. "For as many of you as were baptized into Christ have put on Christ" (Gal 3:27). When we were baptized, he filled us with "living water" (his divine life) and "clothed" us with his enduring love. Just as a branch cannot bear fruit of itself, neither can we, unless we are nourished with his living water and clothed with Christ.

For many reasons, baptism is rightly considered the most important sacrament. Its fruits are bountiful. It adds a divine dimension to our humanness by making us the temple of the living God. We become the adopted sons and daughters of the Father. It conditions us to receive the other sacraments. By Christ's indwelling we become

Christians in a real sense. When an adult receives this sacrament, it cleanses away all sinfulness.

PRUNED TO BEAR GOOD FRUIT

As branches on the Vine, which is Christ, we are to produce fruit as we journey through life. Burdened by our human frailties, we stand in need of constant pruning if we are to be productive branches and bear the fruit the Lord expects of us. Being subjected to this pruning process does not imply that we are not bearing fruit, or that the Father is displeased with us, but that we need to be pruned to bear even more fruit.

The Holy Spirit actively seeks to expose and rid us of those areas of our failure or sin that hold us back from all that God wants us to be and do. How graciously the Lord provides all the means we need to be forgiven and healed, that we may bear more fruit by accomplishing what he asks of us. The two primary channels of forgiveness and healing, of conversion and transformation, are found in the sacraments of Reconciliation and the Eucharist.

As we begin to reflect on our waywardness, we ask the Holy Spirit to enlighten our minds and hearts, that we might be able to acknowledge the faults, shortcomings and sins which prevent us from producing an abundance of good fruit. The Spirit will not only illumine our minds and hearts, but will grant us all the grace we need to walk the way of life to which we are called. An honest examination of conscience, made regularly, is an important step in the process of seeking a real conversion and transformation.

Jesus invites us to meet him in the sacraments of Reconciliation and the Eucharist that he may free us from all our infidelities. These two channels of forgiveness and healing enable us to become fruit-bearing branches. And if we find letting go difficult, the Lord rreminds us, "My grace is sufficient for you, for my power is made perfect in weakness" (2 Cor 12:9). The Lord cannot be outdone in generosity; his sacramental grace will accompany us every step of the way that we may remain firmly attached to him as the branch on the vine.

Another potential means at our fingertips for becoming and remaining a fruitful branch is prayer, especially contemplative prayer, which produces those special fruits we need to live in conformity with the will of the Lord and also to reform our lives to produce even more fruit. Contemplative prayer is a quiet, relaxed, wordless resting in the presence of the Lord. As we keep our focus on him dwelling within us, our interior dispositions begin to change. It is a power-packed prayer that molds and transforms us even though we may not be consciously aware this is taking place within us. Jesus invites us to pray in this way when he bids us, "Remain in my love." As we bask in the sunshine of his love, it will burn away our devious tendencies and energize us to respond more fully to his love. Jesus is happy to assure us, "My Father is glorified by this, that you bear much fruit and become my disciples."

"WITHOUT ME YOU CAN DO NOTHING"

Many of us are saddled with the tendency to pride ourselves on our own ability to succeed in all the undertakings in our daily routine. We like to control and launch out, trusting solely in our own judgment and expertise. If we should fail we become discouraged.

We would do well to recall the caution that Jesus gave us: "Without me you can do nothing." Just as a branch severed from the vine cannot bear fruit, neither can we unless we remain attached to Jesus the Vine. When Jesus warned us that without him we could do nothing, he was also reminding us that with his gifts and grace we could do all things and be fruitful. He does not want us to seek his help only to accomplish what we want to do. The Lord asks us to do his will by living his way of life, not as a duty or obligation, or even to avoid his displeasure or punishment, but rather because we love him and want to do what pleases him. Our primary motivation should always spring from love.

RESPOND TO GOD'S LOVE

So that love might be our primary motivation, Jesus assures us of the enduring love of God hovering over us at all times. "As the Father has loved me, so have I loved you; abide in my love" (Jn 15:9). The Father loves Jesus with an infinite love. In turn, Jesus assures us that he loves us with that same unconditional love, regardless of who we are or what we have done.

Love by its very nature is mutual; it needs a loving response, otherwise it is a rejected love. Genuine love yearns to be present, to please, to assist, to give without counting the cost. We prove our love for God by striving to fulfill his will in all the eventualities of the day. Love not only makes the routine duties and daily demands more tolerable, but blesses us with peace and a sense of fulfillment.

Jesus spells out his way: "If you keep my commandments, you will abide in my love" (Jn 15:10). When Jesus uses the word "commandments," he is not referring merely to the decalogue, but to whatever God asks us to accept and do. The secret to success: "Abide in my love."

Wonder of wonders, mystery of mysteries, our feeble efforts to fulfill God's will and follow Jesus' way of life glorify the Father: "By this my Father is glorified, that you bear much fruit, and so prove to be my disciples" (Jn 15:8).

For Reflection

The profound mystery of our dwelling in Christ, as a branch receiving life from the vine, makes us very special to the Lord. St. Peter reminds us: "You are a chosen race, a royal priesthood, a holy nation, a people of his own, so that we may announce the praises of him who called us out of darkness into his wonderful light" (1 Pet 2:9). Ask yourself:

- How do I respond and cooperate with his divine life and love within me?
- What kind of fruit am I producing: wild grapes, mediocre fruit or a plentiful harvest?
- Do I remind myself that the fruit the Lord expects of me is not feverish activity but a striving for a deeper and more personal union with him?
- How frequently do I pause to thank and praise the Lord for choosing me to be a branch on the True Vine?
- Do I realize that my efforts to bear good fruit give glory to my Father in heaven?

CHAPTER ELEVEN

"I Am the Bread of Life."

THE DESIRE OF EVERY HUMAN HEART is to be accepted and appreciated, to love and to be loved. Much of what we do is done to express our love for another person, or to win the approval and love of a person we cherish. The origin of true love is God. Love is the source of our happiness and joy. It energizes us to reach out in loving concern for others. Genuine love generates total trust and confidence in those we love.

The yearning of every human being is to be accepted and loved by God our Father. Throughout the Old Testament, he reminds us repeatedly of how precious we are to him, how much he loves us just as we are. Jesus, too, loves us with that same unconditional love. Throughout his earthly sojourn, he manifested his boundless love for us in countless ways.

Genuine love must give to the extent of its intensity. Jesus loves us so much that he gave us the greatest gift possible—the gift of himself in the Holy Eucharist. Let us reflect on the words of the extravagant promise he made to us.

I am the bread of life; he who comes to me shall not hunger, and he who believes in me shall never thirst. But I said to you that you have seen me and yet do not believe. All that the Father gives me will come to me; and him who comes to me I will not cast out. For I have come down from heaven, not to do my own will, but the will of him who sent me; and this is the will of him who sent me, that I should lose nothing of all that he has given me, but raise it up at the last day. For this is the will of my Father, that every one who sees the Son and believes in him should have eternal life; and I will raise him up at the last day. **John 6:35-40**

JESUS, MIRACLE WORKER AND "BREAD OF LIFE"

I am the bread of life; he who comes to me shall not hunger, and he who believes in me shall never thirst.

John 6:35

When Jesus spoke these words, he was not speaking merely about physical hunger and thirst, but was assuring us that he could satisfy our every need, be it spiritual, emotional or physical. In him we will find encouragement, comfort, peace, fulfillment and, above all, love. At Mass we come to him to be renewed and filled with all his blessings to satisfy our hunger and thirst for him.

By proclaiming himself the "Bread of Life," Jesus was fulfilling the prophetic images of the Old Testament. The Israelites wandering in the desert were sustained by the God-given manna, a prophetic symbol of the Eucharist. The Lord said to Moses, "Behold, I will rain bread from heaven for you" (Ex 16:4).

Later the psalmist recalls the providential love of God. "And he rained down upon them manna to eat, and gave them the grain of heaven" (Ps 78:24). Melchizedek's offering of bread and wine also prefigured the gift of the Lord himself in the Eucharist (Gen 14:18).

Jesus also demonstrated the truth of his words by his actions in the New Testament. Jesus prepared his followers for the tremendous gift of himself in the Eucharist through several miraculous deeds.

Wedding feast in Cana. At the wedding feast in Cana, Jesus changed water into wine, not only to manifest his divine power but also to reveal the empathy and compassion of his heart. This first miracle of Jesus was also a preparation for the Eucharist. He wanted his followers and us to realize that just as he changed water into wine, he could also, by his Eucharistic presence, change the mediocrity of our life into the sparkling wine of his divine life which he shares with us.

Loaves and fishes. In John's Gospel (6:1-15), Jesus promised us the gift of himself in the Eucharist. He first demonstrated not only his divine power over bread, but also his loving care for every human being.

When a large crowd followed Jesus up the mountain to listen to his teaching, they had no food and were far removed from any place that could supply enough food for such a large crowd. When Jesus learned that they had five barley loaves and two fish, he gave thanks and had the disciples distribute the bread to the crowd of five thousand. The proof of the miracle was the discovery that they had more left over than they had to begin with.

These two manifestations of Jesus' divine power—changing water into wine and multiplying the loaves and fish—were ideal preparations for the gift of himself under the appearances of bread and wine.

JESUS GIVES US THE EUCHARIST

In the hallowed precincts of the Upper Room, the night before he died, Jesus fulfilled his promise to become our Bread of Life. Before he instituted the Eucharist, he proved once again his loving concern not only for the Twelve but also for us. In a lengthy discourse in John's Gospel (chapters 13-17), Jesus spoke only words of comfort and hope, of encouragement and reassurance, of promise and peace:

> Him who comes to me I will not cast out.... I will raise him up at the last day.   **John 6:37,40**

What more could we ask or desire from such a benevolent God? He knew that we would naturally be concerned about attaining our eternal happiness in heaven. But Jesus' words of comfort assure us that if our lives are lived in conformity with the way Jesus mapped out for us, we can be certain of our eternal union with him.

Even though that Passover in the Upper Room was a somber occasion for Jesus, filled with foreboding and sinister plotting, he did not indulge in any self-pity, nor did he speak about his imminent death. His chief concern was to encourage us in our way of life. Jesus began the sacrificial gift of himself for our redemption by giving us himself in the Holy Eucharist so that we might offer ourselves in union with him.

> And he took bread, and when he had given thanks he broke it and gave it to them, saying, "This is my body which is given for you. Do this in remembrance of me." And likewise the cup after supper, saying, "This cup which is poured out for you is the new covenant in my blood."   **Luke 22:19-20**

His redemptive sacrifice was culminated the next day when he made the ultimate oblation of himself on Calvary for our salvation. His directive to his apostles and their successors was imperative: "Do this in memory of me." In every Mass Jesus continues to offer himself anew with the offering we make of ourselves to the Father.

WHY DID JESUS GIVE US HIMSELF IN THE EUCHARIST?

There are at least four reasons Jesus gave himself to us in the Eucharist:

1. *Jesus loves us and wants to give himself continually to us.* Love must give of itself, and God is love. Love wants to be closely associated with the beloved, to love and be loved, to share the joys and sorrows of life. Loving us with an infinite love, Jesus did not want to leave us. He walks with us every step of the way on our journey through life and into eternity. The night before he died, Jesus gave us a consoling promise: "I will not leave you desolate; I will come to you" (Jn 14:18). Through the Eucharist, Jesus constantly reminds us of his love for us.

2. *The Eucharist is a constant reminder of his indwelling presence in us.* When we were baptized we received the Trinitarian life dwelling within us. Jesus came to dwell within us as a life-long companion. Engrossed as we are in all the demanding pursuits of daily living, we can easily become distracted and oblivious to his abiding spiritual presence. In his gentle consideration of our humanness, Jesus gave us the Eucharist, a tangible sign and symbol, as a powerful reminder of his dwelling with us and within us, and also as a means of increasing our faith.

3. *It is a unique dimension of himself.* Our purpose in life is to offer ourselves with all our thoughts, words and activity to the Lord as a gift of self. In the Eucharist Jesus gives us a privileged means of adding a unique dimension to our gift of himself. The Mass affords us an extraordinary opportunity to offer all that we are and do to the Father. In the Mass Jesus devised a way and means, a privileged prerogative, for us to be in such direct communication with the transcendent God of heaven and earth.

4. *It is a channel of divine reconciliation.* Jesus gave us the Eucharist as a channel of reconciliation. In every Mass we meet him as our merciful, compassionate God who is eager to forgive all our faults and sinfulness. As our divine Healer, he also touches every area of our life, healing us of resentments, judgmental attitudes, self-centeredness, and a host of other faults and shortcomings.

THE EUCHARISTIC CELEBRATION

We begin the Mass with the Penitential Rite pausing to beg his forgiveness, especially for our principal failing. Throughout the Eucharistic Celebration, other pleas for mercy and forgiveness are incorporated, making it a source of genuine peace and pardon.

In the Eucharistic Celebration, Jesus invites us to bring the gift of ourselves symbolized by the bread and wine. At times our gift of self may be half-hearted, self-centered, distracted or even reluctant. Jesus accepts our gift as it is presented, unites it to the gift of himself, and offers it to the Father in our name. Even though our offering of self is far from perfect, Jesus adds a new and divine dimension to it by uniting it to the gift of himself.

In preparing the oblation of ourselves we are to conform

as much as possible to the image of Jesus. This is the gift that pleases the Father. It is the image of Jesus formed in us, which the Father graciously accepts with the offering of Jesus. When Jesus commanded us to "do this in memory of me," he was inviting us to put on his mind, his heart and his attitudes so that our lifestyle would conform more and more to his. He admonishes us: "Take my yoke upon you, and learn from me; for I am gentle and lowly in heart" (Mt 11:29).

JESUS SHOWS US THE WAY

Jesus never asks us to do anything which he himself has not done. He shows us the way; he is our exemplar. From the first moment of his birth in Bethlehem to his last gasp on the cross, Jesus gave himself totally to the Father. Jesus lived according to a single precept, which is found in the Book of Hebrews: "Behold, I come to do your will, O God" (Heb 10:7).

Jesus set the pace for us. Unless we make our own self-giving in union with the generous self-giving of Jesus, the Mass with its words, prayers, gestures and postures remains void of any real meaning and bears even less fruit.

MARY, OUR MODEL

Jesus gave us his Mother to be our model in living the Mass throughout each day. Like her Son, Mary dedicated and consecrated her whole life to God, to be used in any capacity he wished. Her journey began in her tender years as the Holy Spirit molded and transformed her sinless soul in preparation for her unique mission in life. Her total devotion was obvious at the time of the Annunciation when she accepted her vocation at great risk. It culminated with the oblation of herself united with her Son on Calvary which concluded the first Mass offered. Mary's dedication and commitment was total and enduring. She never wavered or reneged in giving herself.

As the Mother of the Church and our Mother, Mary continues to offer herself in the Eternal Now of God as she unites herself with the gift we make of ourselves each time we celebrate the Eucharist.

For Reflection

Jesus says to us: "I have invited you to offer me the gift of yourself so that I can fill you with my divine life and love. This is what I meant when I said 'Do this in memory of me.' Let me ask you:

- "When you join me in offering the Mass, do you offer yourself halfheartedly, passively, merely out of a sense of duty or at times even reluctantly?

- "Do you try to prepare yourself beforehand by prayerfully reading my Word in the Scriptures of the Mass, or do you take time to call to mind the privileged mystery in which you are involved?

- "Do you listen attentively to the homily in order to remember a thought or word which might inspire you throughout the day?

- "Do you pause to say 'Thank you' for the tremendous blessings I shower upon you at each Mass?"

CHAPTER TWELVE

"Do You Also Wish to Go Away?"

WE CAN READILY IMAGINE how eager Jesus was to announce that, as the Bread of Life, he would supply all our needs. He promised never to reject anyone who comes to him, but to raise us up on the last day. As we ponder his words, we too are elated to receive these reassurances of his love.

Jesus came into the world to teach us the way to eternal salvation. He taught us to love God by fulfilling his will graciously and to love our neighbor treating him or her as we ourselves want to be accepted and loved. Jesus was well aware of our weak human nature, and that on our own we could never live up to the way of life he had mapped out for us. For this reason he devised a way to live with us and within us, assisting us by his Eucharistic Presence to fulfill all his directives.

However, when Jesus promised his disciples the magnanimous gift of himself in the Eucharist, his words were greeted with an extremely disappointing reaction. Unrest and murmuring stirred throughout the crowd, which was eventually voiced in disbelief: "This is a hard saying; who can listen to it?" (Jn 6:60). Next we hear those heartrending words in John's Gospel: "After this many of his disciples drew back and no longer went about with him" (6:66). Many have regarded these words as the saddest in the Bible.

Try to fathom the pain in the heart of Jesus as he watched them turn away and leave. As the Bread of Life, he had given them all the means they needed to obtain eternal life, if only they believed. But they refused "and no longer accompanied him."

With sad eyes reflecting his disappointment, Jesus turned to the apostles and said, "Do you also wish to go away?" Jesus risked losing these special followers of his, if they would not in faith accept his promise.

There was probably a tense moment as they looked at each other and waited for one of them to respond. Peter broke that awkward silence with a profession of faith which brought some consolation to Jesus: "Lord, to whom shall we go? You have the words of eternal life; and we have believed, and have come to know that you are the Holy One of God" (6:68-69).

WHY BELIEVERS TODAY LEAVE THE EUCHARIST

In spite of the Lord's abiding presence with us in the Eucharist, there are many who no longer go about with him. They offer various reasons and rationalizations for no longer joining Jesus in the Eucharist. They may voice countless excuses that ultimately arise from a lack of faith, a spirit of indifference, a dearth of knowledge or a lack of understanding and appreciation of this tremendous mystery. Their reactions can be summarized in the words of some who had listened to Jesus: "This saying is hard; who can accept it?"

It would be virtually impossible to look at all the reasons given for leaving the sacramental life of the Church but there seem to be two major reasons why some people no longer accompany Jesus: a crisis in faith and a disregard for the important role of community in the act of worship.

CRISIS IN FAITH

Many today abandon the Lord's way of life because they lack an understanding of the Catholic faith. There seems to be wholesale illiteracy about the truths set forth by Jesus, relayed to us in his Word and presented by his Church. For many, their Catholic education has not extended beyond their elementary or high school days. They have little or no adult understanding of Scripture, doctrine or the moral teaching of Jesus.

Some who are experiencing this crisis in faith continue to go to Sunday Mass, often out of a sense of duty or obligation. They no longer appreciate what a wonderful privilege we have to offer ourselves—all that we do and are—to the Father, along with the offering of Jesus, and to praise and thank our heavenly Father for his bountiful gifts. The tremendous mystery of the Mass escapes their understanding. However, we are reminded of this mystery in every Mass as the celebrant or deacon invites us to "proclaim the mystery of faith: Christ has died, Christ is risen, Christ will come again."

We cannot love a person we do not know, and we cannot know a person to whom we have not listened with our heart. A deeper understanding of the mystery of the Eucharist will bring us to a richer appreciation of the Lord's gift to us and our unique privilege of being able to unite ourselves with him and with his whole Body, the Church.

Return to the Upper Room. Gathered with his apostles in the Upper Room for the Last Supper, Jesus was about to give them the very special gift that he had prepared during his sojourn with them, the gift of himself in the Holy Eucharist.

How brief and unembellished are the recorded words Jesus spoke to change bread and wine into his own Body and Blood: "Take, eat; this is my body" (Mt 26:26). Raising the cup, he said, "Drink of it, all of you; for this is my blood of the covenant, which is poured out for many for the forgiveness of sins" (v. 27-28). Jesus' command, "Do this in memory of me," (see 1 Corinthians 11:24) enables us to get a little glimpse into the profound mystery of the Eucharist.

Jesus' request is brief, direct and imperative, but there is much more contained in the words than the translation seems to imply, especially in the word *memory*. A better understanding of what is really meant by memory will help us get a better insight into the tremendous mystery in the Sacrifice of the Mass.

"In memory of Me..." Those who are bilingual sometimes feel a certain sense of frustration when trying to translate a special meaning or nuance of a word from one language to another. At times there are no words in the second language that express the precise meaning of an original phrase or idiom.

We encounter this same difficulty when we try to translate or grasp exactly what Jesus really meant when he said, "Do this in memory of me." This instruction of Jesus is often interpreted too narrowly. Jesus was not referring only to the words of consecration. He meant much more.

The word *memory* is the key to a better understanding of what is implied in the directive of Jesus. In our usage, memory means a calling to mind of some event or happening of the past. As Jesus used the word *memory*, it meant making the reality of the past present in the here and now.

How is this possible? We must step into the realm of the supernatural. Here we do not see things as God sees them. We live in time and space. We see events naturally in the course of time—one event following upon another then passing into history. But God is not confined to time and space. He lives in an Eternal Now. All that ever happened and all that will ever happen is present to God at every moment.

With this concept in mind, we can reflect on the Sacrifice of the Mass and discover a whole new dimension in the Eucharistic Celebration. When Jesus offered his redemptive sacrifice, begun at the Last Supper and culminating on the cross, his sacrifice entered into God's Eternal Now to be present until the end of time. When we celebrate the Eucharist, we relive, re-present and recall with Jesus his suffering and death. It is a mystical celebration reminding us of his infinite love for us: "Greater love has no man than this, that a man lay down his life for his friends" (Jn 15:13). As we celebrate the Mass, we renew our praise and gratitude for his redeeming love. As we pray the Mass, it helps us recall the tremendous price he paid for our sinfulness and should deter us from succumbing to temptation. Our whole purpose in life is to offer ourselves with all that we think, do and say to the Lord. The oblation of Jesus urges us to renew our own offering of self in union with him because we are the Body of Christ.

The Eternal Now of the family of God. In the Eternal Now, when Jesus offered himself on Calvary, he was not alone. The whole Body of Christ was there: everyone who was ever baptized and everyone who will ever be baptized was there. You and I were there, uniting ourselves with his self-giving. The love, praise and thanksgiving which we bring to Mass was and will be present in every Mass that will ever be offered to the Father.

When we unite ourselves with Jesus, our eternal high priest, we enter into communion with every person who ever was and with every person who ever will be. What a tremendous song of praise and thanksgiving resounds in heaven as we enter into the Eternal Now of God. The fruits of our joining with the whole Body of Christ are extraordinary. When we pray at Mass, even for our private personal intentions, the whole Body of Christ prays with us and for us, adding immense power to our prayer.

When we offer the Eucharist, we are spiritually present and united with Mary, our Mother. We were united with her as she stood near the cross of her dying Son and made her oblation along with his. When we offer Mass she is present with us, interceding with and for us, praising and thanking God with us.

We form one body with all the saints who ever lived and ever will live. In a very real sense, we join all our loved ones: those whom the Lord has already called to their eternal reward, as well as those who are still with us in this land of exile, and even those yet unborn.

Try to fathom the full implication of the Eternal Now of God. It is a great mystery. When the celebrant utters those powerful words of the Master, "Do this in memory of me," he is proclaiming a baffling mystery. This is why immediately after the Consecration, we are invited by the priest or deacon to express our belief in this wonderful mystery, "Let us proclaim the mystery of faith." May our profession of faith be pleasing to the Lord and with his inspiration may it radiate and stimulate the faith of others.

MASS IS A COMMUNITY ACT OF WORSHIP

Another major reason why so many wander away from the Church and no longer participate in its sacramental life stems from a grave lack of understanding of the Mass as a community act of worship. I sometimes hear comments such as "I do not need to go to Mass since I can worship at home and say all my prayers even better than in Church." Some people complain that the Mass does not help them meet the demands and problems of everyday living. They are not able to integrate the Mass into their daily lives.

These and similar comments may arise because, to some extent, we have lost the community aspect of the Eucharistic Celebration. Many have attended Mass while regarding it only as a duty and a time for private devotions. The attitude behind each of the statements mentioned above indicates that the community aspect of Mass is not fully understood and appreciated.

Early Christian community. In the primitive Church, the first Christians formed a closely knit community. They were criticized, isolated, misunderstood and persecuted, which caused them to form support groups. In these groups the early Christians found great mutual encouragement from each other and strong supernatural help in the Eucharistic community. St. Luke records this fact in the Acts of the Apostles: "And they devoted themselves to the apostles' teaching and fellowship, to the breaking of bread and the prayers" (Acts 2:42). Within the Eucharistic community they found the inspiration and motivation to implement the love of neighbor that Jesus made so imperative for their Christian way of life. Recall the badge of the early Christians: "See, how they love one another."

THE LITURGY'S INFLUENCE ON OUR SENSE OF COMMUNITY

In the centuries that followed the initial founding of the early Church, this genuine sense of community began to wane. So did the rich appreciation and understanding of the Mass as a worshipping community. Gradually a custom developed among the worshippers that while present at Mass, they should take that time to worship the Lord privately as isolated members of the congregation. The appreciation of *community*—the coming together as the family of God—soon faded. A number of factors in the liturgy and in society contributed to the decline in the sense of community worship.

Changes in social living had effects on the Christian community. For centuries lay people fulfilled a number of offices in the Church, such as lectors, porters, exorcists and acolytes. With the advent of the Industrial Age in the seventeenth century, many of the faithful were no longer able to fulfill these functions in the liturgy. Bound by the factory work schedule, they were not always free to participate in the church's worship. When this occurred, the church introduced Minor Orders and ordained certain people to fulfill these duties. The lack of participation in the communal worship contributed to the loss of a sense of community. Today as lay people are participating more fully in these liturgical functions, the Minor Orders have been discontinued.

Other aspects of the liturgy were destructive to the sense of community and spawned the notion of the Mass as a time for private devotions.

The priest's celebrating Mass by facing the altar with his back toward the congregation was intended as a sign of leading the people to the Lord. However, it tended to remove the celebrant from the people and failed to emphasize the oneness of a community united in going to the Lord.

When Mass was offered in Latin, it was done to show the universality of the Church as she spread into different countries. Since most of the people did not know Latin, and could not understand the prayers, they used the occasion to "get in their own prayers."

After the Reformation, when the Eucharistic Presence was reserved in churches, the tabernacle was frequently broken into by the enemies of the Church and the consecrated hosts were desecrated. To prevent this desecration, a high protective screen was erected to prevent any unauthorized person from entering the sanctuary. When this danger passed and the screen was no longer needed, the communion rail became a remnant of the protective screen. However, the rail also added to the impression of separation between the priest and people.

As the populace lost its sense of communal worship, other private devotions began to spring up. People used the time of Mass to say their rosary and other personal prayers. As they developed a private relationship with the Eucharistic Lord, it blinded them to the community dimension of the Mass. They attended Mass to obtain help in their difficulties, to present their own personal needs to the Lord and to build up a store of graces and blessings for themselves. All these practices are commendable, but they are not conducive to understanding and appreciating the Mass as communal worship.

RESTORING OUR SENSE OF COMMUNITY

In the Second Vatican Council the bishops, working under the guidance of the Holy Spirit, saw the great need to reintroduce a sense of community into the Eucharistic Celebration. They understood the need to move from a private, devotional and individualistic approach to the Mass to a communal understanding of it. This movement would be a powerful means for forming genuine Christian community.

Liturgical Changes. To refocus our attention on the communal importance of the Mass, many liturgical changes have been introduced. These are avenues to greater participation for all who come to offer the Eucharist. All the prayers of the Mass are said in the vernacular, enabling all the worshippers to understand and to respond to them. Lectors now proclaim the Word of God and lead the congregation in responding to his Word. The celebrant faces the congregation, which unites him more closely to the people. Bringing the gifts of bread and wine in the offertory procession to the celebrant reminds the people to make their own oblation to the Lord. Community singing and responses, especially to the prayers of the faithful, add another dimension to the awareness of community. Receiving Communion in the hand is a symbolic gesture reminding us of our mission to bring the Lord to others.

Of course, these external liturgical changes are commendable, but they cannot of themselves restore a genuine sense of Christian community. Real Christian community cannot be formed by rules and regulations alone. Authentic community must spring from the heart. It is founded on love of God, love of neighbor and love of self. Following the guidelines of the Second Vatican Council, the Church is striving to bring us to a deeper appreciation of genuine Christian community, showing us how the Mass can be a powerful instrument in forming a loving, caring, concerned community.

Forgiveness as a means for restoring community. An important step in striving to achieve a loving community spirit is learning to forgive one another. This forgiveness must be extended to the members of our own natural family as well as the members of the family of God—the Body of Christ. To forgive another person may be difficult at times, but it is essential. Jesus made it a necessary condition for offering the Eucharist worthily:

If you bring your gift to the altar, and there recall that your brother has anything against you, leave your gift there at the altar, go first and be reconciled with your brother, and then come and offer your gift.

Matthew 5:23-24

Jesus told Peter that we must forgive seventy times seven, which means always. In teaching us the Lord's Prayer, the words of Jesus leave little doubt about the necessity for us to forgive: "And forgive us our debts, as we also have forgiven our debtors" (Mt 6:12). We pray these words each time we offer the Eucharist. What a powerful lesson Jesus taught us from his agony on the cross. He pleaded, "Father, forgive them; for they know not what they do" (Lk 23:34). Jesus not only prayed for forgiveness, but he even excused them as he does us.

The Church has included in every Mass a brief ceremony, the penitential rite, which can be very effective in removing barriers that obstruct good interpersonal relationships. After the opening greeting at Mass, the celebrant invites the congregation to recall their sinfulness and in silence to ask for forgiveness and healing. Before the solemn moment of communion, we pause to extend a prayerful wish to others by offering a sign of peace. This brief prayerful wish is a petition asking for all God's blessings upon another person, especially the blessing of eternal salvation. This is the full meaning of the *Shalom* which Jesus used. It is also a way of fostering and healing interpersonal relationships.

Prayer and the Church community. Praying with others has a real bonding power and helps form genuine Christian community. At Mass we do not pray in isolation, but with the whole Body of Christ worshipping and praying with us. Jesus, the principal offerer of the Mass, is praying with us and for us. Uniting our prayers with those of the whole community adds a greater dimension and power to our own prayer. For instance, if we wish to thank and praise God for a special favor we have received, it is good to know that a myriad of voices and hearts join us in celebrating the goodness of the Lord. Likewise, our petitions are raised to the Lord by all the members of the community.

A priest friend said that when he is offering Mass, before he begins the "Gloria," he invites the congregation to praise and glorify God with all the Christians around the world: "It thrills me to realize that I am praising God with every member of the Body of Christ, both those here on earth and those making up the whole host of heaven. What a privilege to add my weak voice with the whole family of God!"

The petitions found in the Eucharistic prayers of the Mass are a powerful means of establishing genuine Christian community. They are addressed to the Holy Spirit, the very source of love, unity and peace—essential ingredients for forming community. Although Eucharistic prayers may vary, our prayer to the Holy Spirit is always the same plea for genuine Christian community in the Body of Christ:

"May all of us who share in the body and blood of Christ be brought together in unity by the Holy Spirit."

"Grant that we, who are nourished by his body and blood, may be filled with the Holy Spirit and become one body and one spirit in Christ."

"By your Holy Spirit, gather all who share this one bread and one cup into one body of Christ, a living sacrifice of praise."

Praying together as a community has a bonding power beyond any other force. As we worship together, a solidarity and a spiritual unity is formed which cannot be found elsewhere. Prayer has such a power. Worshipping together at Mass as the family of God will satisfy many of our needs. As we celebrate the Eucharist in a community, we discover that we are accepted and appreciated by others, which is the desire of every human heart.

Our prayer of petition and praise at Mass takes on an unlimited dimension since we are raising our hearts and voices, not only with our brothers and sisters, but with the principal Offerer himself, Jesus, our eternal high priest. Remember that Jesus promised: "Whatever you ask in my name, I will do it.." (Jn 14:13).

The role of community in evangelism. The true spirit of community that is generated at Mass is not confined to the time of worship only. It will make us more apostolic, empathetic and concerned about others. At the close of every Mass the celebrant sends us forth to radiate the love, peace and joy of the Lord to everyone who comes into our lives. This commissioning is expressed both in Scripture and in the liturgy itself: "Go in peace to love and serve the Lord."

When we experience more fully the blessings of the community aspect of Mass, our response to the question, "Do you also wish to go away?" will no doubt echo Peter's response, "Lord, to whom shall we go? You have the words of eternal life" (Jn 6:67-68).

≈≈≈

For Reflection

As we pause to examine our thoughts, feelings and attitudes about going to Mass, we may discover some areas of neglect on our part or a lack of appreciation of the great privilege which is ours. We will also enrich our gratitude for the unique mystery of love in which we can participate. Attempting to respond to the following questions will be helpful in making a more accurate survey.

- Do I regard going to Mass only as a duty or obligation giving Jesus cause to ask, "Do you also wish to go away?"

- Do I remind myself that my prayer at Mass is united to the prayers of praise, thanksgiving and petition of the whole Body of Christ, thus giving my prayer an extraordinary dimension and efficacy?

- Do I try to bring myself to a deeper understanding of the Mass as community worship and participate as fully as I can in the liturgical celebration?

- Do I prayerfully ponder the mystery of God's Eternal Now, realizing that I join all the angels and saints in offering redemptive sacrifice in heaven?

- Do I thank God for my gift of faith which enables me to say with Peter, "Lord, to whom shall we go? You have the words of eternal life."

CHAPTER THIRTEEN

"Are You the Christ?"

WHEN THE HIGH PRIEST ASKED JESUS if he were "the Christ, the Son of the Blessed," Jesus answered simply, "I am." With this laconic statement, Jesus declared that he was indeed the Messiah and that every detail foretold about the Messiah by the prophets was being fulfilled in him. Throughout the Old Testament, the prophets clearly described the redemptive suffering and death of the Messiah to come.

In the Garden of Eden, after Adam and Eve had turned away from God, they were not abandoned by God but were promised a Redeemer (Gn 3:15). The Psalms reveal many facts about the coming of the Messiah who would redeem the human race by his suffering and death. Isaiah and Jeremiah speak frequently, and in much detail, about the suffering of the Messiah.

FORESHADOWINGS OF CHRIST
IN THE OLD TESTAMENT

The Old Testament records stories of persons who, by their suffering, foreshadowed or typified the suffering Jesus would endure. Abraham's willingness to sacrifice his only son, Isaac, at God's command prefigures the Father sending Jesus as a victim for our sins. Joseph being sold into slavery by his own brothers was a foreshadowing of Jesus' betrayal. Jeremiah, too, was a figure of the Messiah in the rejection, sufferings and eventual death which he endured.

Hundreds of years before Jesus came into our world, Isaiah, one of the great prophets of the Old Testament, foretold precisely what the Messiah would have to suffer to redeem the human race. Four different times he predicted specific details of what the Messiah would endure, all of which were fulfilled in Jesus. These predictions, found in the book of Isaiah, are called the "Suffering Servant Songs."

"Suffering Servant Songs." A few brief quotes from the fourth Suffering Servant song will give us a glimpse into the prophet's vision. In his prophecy, Isaiah foretold that the Messiah would assume human nature in order to redeem it: "Surely he has borne our griefs and carried our sorrows" (Is 53:4).

The scourging of Jesus was foretold in these words: "With his stripes we are healed" (Is 53:5).

The reason for the Messiah's redemptive suffering was to justify us. The prophet outlines the fruits of Jesus' suffering when he says, "He poured out his soul to death, and was numbered with the transgressors; yet he bore the sin of many, and made intercession for the transgressors" (Is 53:11-12).

JESUS PREDICTS THE DEATH OF THE MESSIAH

Throughout his earthly sojourn, Jesus tried repeatedly to keep his followers aware that the Messiah would suffer and eventually die. All three synoptic Gospels record three separate times in each Gospel the predictions Jesus made about his forthcoming suffering and death. Luke records the third prophecy of Jesus in these words:

> And taking the twelve, he said to them, "Behold, we are going up to Jerusalem, and everything that is written of the Son of man by the prophets will be accomplished. For he will be delivered to the Gentiles, and will be mocked and shamefully treated and spit upon; they will scourge him and kill him, and on the third day he will rise."
> **Luke 18:31-33**

The disciples protested. His disciples simply could not comprehend the idea that Jesus would be persecuted, rejected and condemned to death. They remembered how he had eluded his enemies on various occasions: When the Jewish leaders had tried to throw him off a cliff at Nazareth, Jesus walked through their midst without a hand being laid upon him. When the temple guards were sent to arrest him as he was teaching in the temple, they were rendered powerless. Jesus' followers were convinced that surely Jesus would again escape any attempt to punish him or take him into custody.

On one occasion when Jesus spoke about the fate which awaited him, Peter vehemently protested. Jesus sternly admonished him, "Get behind me, Satan! You are a hindrance to me; for you are not on the side of God, but of men" (Mt 16:23). Peter's refusal to accept the possibility of Jesus' suffering was an attempt on the part of the devil to deflect Jesus from fulfilling the Father's plan of redemption.

The Jewish leaders rejected him. The followers of Jesus had difficulty imagining a suffering Messiah; the Jewish leaders could not have accepted the concept of a rejected, condemned Messiah any more readily. They visualized the Messiah as a powerful conqueror and liberator. St. Paul frequently speaks about these false expectations when he refers to the paradox of the cross. He writes: "For Jews demand signs and Greeks seek wisdom, but we preach Christ crucified, a stumbling block to Jews and folly to Gentiles" (1 Cor 1:22ff).

Jesus the Messiah. During his sojourn on earth, Jesus fulfilled every detail the prophets foretold about him, especially in his suffering and death. However, Jesus seldom referred to himself as "Messiah" because Jews of that day had false notions of what the word meant.

Some were expecting a great political leader who would restore the golden age of the Davidic kingdom. They had high hopes and great expectations of becoming a powerful nation. Others were expecting a mighty warrior who would free them from the slavery and domination of the Romans. They too had ambitions of becoming a great nation, perhaps even a world power as the chosen people.

Jewish authorities threatened to excommunicate anyone who recognized Jesus as the Messiah—yet another reason why Jesus did not want anyone to call him the Messiah. Jewish authorities and many of the people could not conceive of a Messiah who would redeem mankind by laying down his life for the salvation of the world. They were not looking for a suffering servant but a powerful leader. For all these reasons Jesus did not refer to himself as the Messiah but as the "Son of David" or the "Son of Man."

Only twice in the Gospels did Jesus admit that he was the Messiah. During his lengthy discussion with the Samaritan woman, Jesus enkindled the seed of faith in her heart. She responded, "I know that the Messiah is coming (he who is called Christ); when he comes, he will show us all things." Jesus said to her, "I who speak to you am he" (Jn 4:25-26). Because this woman was not a Jew, Jesus could speak freely to her without risking her excommunication, which is what happened to any Jew who confessed

Jesus as the Messiah.

The second time Jesus admitted that he was the Messiah was during his trial before the Sanhedrin. Throughout their questioning and despite the false accusations brought against him, Jesus remained silent and offered no defense. He answered only those questions which the high priest had a right to ask. When the high priest asked him, "Are you the Christ, the Son of the Blessed?" Jesus did not hesitate but answered loud and clear, thereby signing his own death warrant:

"I am; and you will see the Son of man seated at the right hand of Power, and coming with the clouds of heaven." And the high priest tore his garments, and said, "Why do we still need witnesses? You have heard his blasphemy. What is your decision?" And they all condemned him as deserving death.   **Mark 14:61-64**

When Jesus was condemned to death, it was the culmination of an endless series of rejections. At his birth, he was rejected by Herod (Mt 2:13). When Jesus invited the wealthy young man whom he loved to follow him, the young man refused and "went away sorrowful" (Mk 10:22). When Jesus declared himself the Bread of Life, many disciples "no longer went about with him" (Jn 6:66).

We cannot possibly comprehend the pain of rejection Jesus suffered when he began his redemptive passion and death: denied by the apostle he had chosen to lead his Church; betrayed by Judas and sold for thirty pieces of silver; deserted by all of them except John. The physical and emotional suffering was beyond our imagining.

Why a suffering Messiah? There is a great emphasis on the role of Jesus as the suffering Messiah. What motivated Jesus to fulfill the role of the "suffering servant" predicted by

Isaiah? As the suffering Messiah, Jesus fulfilled his mission as Savior and Redeemer of the world. According to the Father's plan, Jesus had to assume our human nature in order to redeem it and restore its capacity to receive his divine life and love, which Paul calls "the newness of life." How clearly Paul explains God's plan of salvation in the Letter to the Romans.

> Do you not know that all of us who have been baptized into Christ Jesus were baptized into his death? We were buried therefore with him by baptism into death, so that as Christ was raised from the dead by the glory of the Father, we too might walk in newness of life.
>
> **Romans 6:3-4**

JESUS, OUR MODEL OF PATIENT SUFFERING

By accepting the rejections and sufferings inflicted upon him, Jesus showed us the way we ought to accept our cup of suffering. Our human nature rebels against pain and afflictions of any kind. We need encouragement to endure peacefully the heartaches, disappointments, frustrations and suffering which accompany us on our journey through life.

By following Jesus as our model, we find the motivation we need to endure suffering with courage and patience. Jesus was silent and uncomplaining when he was criticized, rejected and falsely accused. By his sufferings Jesus gained our eternal salvation; by uniting our sufferings with his, we can more easily walk in his footsteps.

As we contemplate the Person of Jesus, we will come to realize that Jesus proved his love for us beyond any shadow of doubt. Love was the impelling motive in the Father's plan as well as in Jesus' desire to fulfill that salvific plan. The Father loves us so much that he gave himself to us in the

Person of Jesus. He did not abandon us after our sinfulness severed our relationship with him:

> For God so loved the world that he gave his only Son, that whoever believes in him should not perish but have eternal life. For God sent the Son into the world, not to condemn the world, but that the world might be saved through him.   **John 3:16-17**

Jesus declared his unbounded love for us when he said, "Greater love has no man than this, that a man lay down his life for his friends" (Jn 15:13). The very next day, he proved that love when he gasped his last breath on the cross.

Emmaus road. After the resurrection, Jesus confirmed the truth that redemptive and vicarious suffering was the lot of the Messiah. When he met the two downcast disciples on the road to Emmaus, he chided them for their lack of faith in understanding the Scriptures:

> "O foolish men, and slow of heart to believe all that the prophets have spoken! Was it not necessary that the Christ should suffer these things and enter into his glory?" And beginning with Moses and all the prophets, he interpreted to them in all the scriptures the things concerning himself.   **Luke 24:25-27**

These words brought the disciples much reassurance and peace, especially when they recognized him in the breaking of the bread. Later that same day he appeared to all the disciples in Jerusalem and clarified the precise role of the Messiah:

Thus it is written, that the Christ should suffer and on the third day rise from the dead, and that repentance and forgiveness of sins should be preached in his name to all nations. **Luke 24:46**

Jesus pointed out to them that his death was not a defeat of God's plan but rather an exact fulfillment of God's will for the salvation of all mankind. He wanted to remind them that their role was to preach "the forgiveness of sins... in his name to all nations." We are the beneficiaries of that outpouring of divine love.

We will profit greatly and eternally if we can respond affirmatively to the next question Jesus asks: "Can you drink the cup that I drink?" which is the subject of our next chapter.

❦

For Reflection

As we spend quiet time with the Lord, we may experience certain thoughts and feelings about what Jesus, the Messiah, did when he suffered to redeem us. Try to ponder and respond as Jesus asks the following questions:

- Do you realize that I willingly laid down my life to redeem you because I love you so very much I want you to be with me for all eternity?

- Do you trust me when I tell you that not even your slightest suffering is in vain when you unite it to my suffering for the salvation of souls?

- Since I gave the gift of my life for you, do you love me enough to offer me the gift of yourself with all you enjoy as well as all you endure throughout the day?

- Do you try to bring comfort and consolation to those who are suffering physically, emotionally or spiritually?

CHAPTER FOURTEEN

"Are You Able to Drink the Cup That I Drink?"

As THE TEACHING MISSION OF JESUS was drawing to a close, he wanted to prepare his disciples for his ministry of suffering and the ultimate fate which awaited him. All three of the synoptic Gospels (Matthew, Mark and Luke) record the prophecy Jesus made three separate times in each of the Gospels. Jesus' words are recorded here in the Gospel of Mark:

> Behold, we are going up to Jerusalem; and the Son of man will be delivered to the chief priests and the scribes, and they will condemn him to death, and deliver him to the Gentiles and they will mock him, and spit upon him, and scourge him, and kill him; and after three days he will rise. **Mark 10:33-34**

By these pronouncements Jesus was trying to prepare the disciples for the passion and death he would have to undergo to redeem our fallen world. He knew that they would be shocked and scandalized at what might appear to be a devastating defeat and the final end of the kingdom he had promised.

Jesus was very explicit in telling them what would happen. By doing so, he was not indulging in self-pity, nor was he seeking sympathy. He was trying to help his disciples avoid becoming disheartened, discouraged or shattered when they saw him going down in what his enemies considered an utter defeat.

ON THE WAY TO JERUSALEM

As they continued their journey toward Jerusalem after this somber announcement, two of his apostles, James and John, approached Jesus with a request: "Grant us to sit, one at your right hand and one at your left, in your glory" (Mk 10:37).

How disappointing this request must have been for Jesus. They made no comment about the horrible suffering he was about to undergo, no word of support, only a selfish concern for themselves and their personal glory. Jesus did not censure them for their self-centeredness but went on to explain what life held out for them:

> You do not know what you are asking. Are you able to drink the cup that I drink, or to be baptized with the baptism with which I am baptized?   **Mark 10:38**

The cup of which Jesus spoke was the cup of suffering. In the Garden of Gethsemane, Jesus referred to his forthcoming passion and death as a cup: "My Father, if it be possible, let this cup pass from me; nevertheless, not as I will, but as thou wilt" (Mt 26:39). Jesus was referring to a total submersion into the rejection and pain he was about to undergo when he spoke of "the baptism with which I am baptized."

Jesus wanted the disciples to be fully aware of what was in store for them. In a sense Jesus was asking them, "Can you bear to go through the terrible experience which I am about to endure? Can you face being submerged into the hatred, pain, rejection and death which I am about to suffer?" Jesus explained that the glory they were seeking could not be achieved without taking up their crosses and following him. The greatness they desired in the kingdom comes only by the standard of the cross—the patient acceptance of suffering. It is true that in the days to come the disciples would endure suffering, as did their Master before them, and would enter into the glory of heaven.

TAKE UP YOUR CROSS

Jesus asks each of us the same question: "Are you able to drink the cup that I drink, or to be baptized with the baptism with which I am baptized?" He is asking us if we are willing to accept our suffering and unite it along with his for our own salvation and for the salvation of others.

Our human nature cringes at the thought of pain, suffering, hardship and rejection. Our cup of suffering may be emotional, spiritual or physical. All suffering is shrouded in a mystery we cannot comprehend. Great minds throughout the ages have been unable to find a reason or explanation for it. When suffering comes into our life, all we can do is keep our focus on Jesus and beg for the grace and strength to endure it. In doing so, we will find peace in our pain.

Physical suffering. In our human condition, physical suffering is a common experience for almost every person, be it illness, injury or simply fatigue from the daily pressures of life. Illness is the acid test of our humanness. Temporary illness—causing us pain, distress and discomfort—may force us to postpone or cancel carefully planned programs and projects. Longer illness or physical impairment, especially one requiring total dependence on others, may necessitate a change in lifestyle. Physical limitations, including a variety of aches and pains, are often our lot in the later years of life.

While suffering remains a mystery, we can always find comfort and acceptance in the example Jesus set before us. During his earthly sojourn he experienced inhuman physical suffering, but was always submissive to the Father's will. While the cross may be a condition for discipleship, an awareness of the abiding presence with us at all times will mitigate our pain, enable us to accept our condition and bring us peace even though tears may flow.

Emotional suffering. Included in emotional suffering are all the heartaches, disappointments, discouragements, frustrations, misunderstandings, criticisms and rejections we face. It also includes mental suffering: the worries, anxieties, doubts, fears and uncertainties about the future. Many of these we bring on ourselves because of our lack of trust and confidence in God's loving care and concern for every detail of our life. Did not Jesus remind us that our heavenly Father knows all our needs, and that we should first seek his kingdom and righteousness and all these things will be given to us besides (Mt 6:32-33)? Jesus exhorts us, "Let not your hearts be troubled; believe in God, believe also in me" (Jn 14:1).

When misunderstanding, criticism and persecution come our way, Jesus gives us this reassurance: "Blessed are you when men revile you and persecute you and utter all kinds of evil against you falsely on my account. Rejoice and be glad, for your reward is great in heaven" (Mt 5:11-12).

Spiritual suffering. Spiritual suffering may be a dryness in prayer with no sense of the Lord's presence, or a reluctance to spend time in prayer, or frustration when we receive no apparent response from God to our petitions and needs.

We need to remember that no prayer of ours goes unanswered. It may not be at the time or in the way we expect, but the Lord assures us: "Ask, and it will be given you; seek, and you will find; knock, and it will be opened to you" (Mt 7:7).

We can easily become discouraged when we fall again and again into the same faults, bad habits and sinfulness. With St. Paul we lament: "For I do not do the good I want, but the evil I do not want is what I do" (Rom 7:19). If we find ourselves in this state, like St. Paul, we will find great consolation in the forgiving, healing love of the Lord and then with him we can say, "Thanks be to God through Jesus Christ our Lord" (Rom 7:25).

Scrupulosity can be a painful spiritual illness causing endless fretting, anxiety and worry. Developing a deep trust in the Lord's love and having the guidance of a spiritual director are the best antidotes. The Lord is always willing to heal when we approach him with faith and trust.

WHY DOES GOD ALLOW SUFFERING?

When sorrow and affliction come into our lives, God has a specific reason for allowing it—and his own timetable for removing it. If he does not remove it from our lives immediately, he may want us to bear it for a certain period of time. The Lord permits suffering to come in order to transform us until we are ready to let God elevate us to a new and higher level of love and union with him. It is a conditioning process.

A little boy daily passed a sculptor's shop on his way to school. He was intrigued as he peered through the window to watch the sculptor at work. One day he had the courage to go into the shop and watch as the sculptor chiseled away at a large block of marble. The boy was amazed to discover the head of a lion emerging from the block of marble. He asked the sculptor, "How did you know the lion was in there?"

Similarly, the Lord chisels away at our faults, bad habits and shortcomings by means of the sufferings he permits to come into our lives. Suffering helps us keep our focus on the Lord. As we contemplate him, we become more and more like him as we put on his mind and heart.

Does God send evil into our lives? God is never the author of evil, but sorrow and affliction are not necessarily evil. If they come from the Lord, they are always for our good, not just for eternity but also for here and now. According to St. Augustine, God could in no wise permit the kind of evil out of which he could not bring good. St. Paul also encourages us when he says, "I consider that the sufferings of this present time are not worth comparing with the glory that is to be revealed to us" (Rom 8:18).

Asking why a good God allows evil does not enable us to understand suffering, or to bear it any better. We must humbly accept the fact that our good and loving God permits suffering. It is through this gift of suffering that our fallen human nature can be elevated and we can live holier lives. In suffering we develop a sure foundation for a deeper spiritual life, a life in union with God, founded on genuine humility.

A cross, not a crisis. If we wish to be a friend and follower of Jesus, the cross will be the means by which we develop a rich, personal relationship with him. Jesus himself announced the role of the cross in our spiritual growth: "If any man would come after me, let him deny himself and take up his cross daily and follow me" (Lk 9:23). The cross embraces all the happenings in our lives, the pleasant as well as the painful.

Our own attitude will make a great difference in the

severity of the pain we experience. At times we may be distressed because we cannot function as we normally would, or we may be miserable since our control over life's situations is limited when some affliction falls to our lot. With the help of God's grace, we can strive to accept whatever comes our way. Only then will we discover a calm and serenity leading us into genuine peace.

Our quiet, calm acceptance of suffering is pleasing to the Lord, since it is the means whereby our life is directed more fully to what he wants us to be. It is a process of growth and maturation in our spiritual life. This will not always be easy; many times we will have to smile through our tears. The Lord understands our humanness and asks only for an honest effort on our part. We will enjoy peace and fulfillment to the extent that we are able to say yes to the Lord. When suffering is united with the passion of Jesus and his redemptive death, it has great value for the individual, for the Church and for society.

I once visited two patients in a nursing home on the same day. The first one was an elderly man whose illness was terminal. He was bitter and angry at God. He was very explicit in voicing his bitterness. When I asked if I could pray with him, he refused in no uncertain terms. I left with a heavy heart.

The second patient I visited was in a similar physical condition, but with a totally different attitude. She had no family or friends to visit her. When I asked if she ever was lonely, she smiled, reached to her bedside table and produced a tattered picture of the Good Shepherd and said, "He is always with me."

The threefold secret to patient forbearance. Scripture outlines a threefold program which will make all suffering more tolerable. The apostle Paul urges us:

Rejoice in your hope,
be patient in tribulation,
be constant in prayer.   **Romans 12:12**

As we strive to make these directives our guidelines when difficulties, hardships and suffering plague us, we will find acceptance more palatable.

But I don't want to suffer! No one ever wanted or welcomed suffering, not even Jesus. In the Garden of Gethsemane, when he envisioned the dreadful pain and the apparent futility of his suffering, he cried out, "Father, if thou art willing, remove this cup from me; nevertheless not my will, but thine, be done" (Lk 22:42). On another occasion Jesus advised, "For I have given you an example, that you also should do as I have done to you" (Jn 13:15).

What does Mary teach us about suffering? The little we know about the life of Mary, the Mother of Jesus and our Mother, charts a course for us to follow in all the afflictions in life. Even though her heart and will were perfectly in tune with the will of God, her sufferings were especially painful. Her sinlessness gave her deeper insights into the hatred, rejection and pain her Son suffered, which intensified her own suffering.

On Calvary, she made her total oblation along with that of Jesus. She is our Mother of Sorrows and is a perfect model for us in times of distress.

Mary's advice to the attendants at the wedding feast in Cana, "Do whatever he tells you," enabled Jesus to work his first miracle of changing water into wine. As our Mother, she encourages us also to "Do whatever he tells you," so that her Son may work miracles of grace in our hearts.

When Jesus asks us, "Are you able to drink the cup that I drink?" may our response be the same as that of James and John: "We can, with your grace and ever-confirming love."

❧

For Reflection

Jesus is well aware that in our humanness we cringe at the very thought of suffering, pain or rejection. His own passion and death is an example for us. He also promises that no suffering of ours is in vain; it will bring untold blessings both here and hereafter. To respond to Jesus' question, I need to ask myself:

- How do I accept my daily cross?

- Do I accept instruction, criticism and misunderstanding quietly and gracefully?

- Has distress caused me to complain, become irritable and impatient, to indulge in self-pity or even become angry?

- Do I unite my sufferings with the sufferings of Jesus for the salvation of souls?

- Do I try to accept suffering patiently as Mary, our Sorrowful Mother, did throughout her life on earth?

CHAPTER FIFTEEN

"I Am the Resurrection and the Life."

A MINISTER ONCE THOUGHT HE SAW A MAN dozing during the sermon and decided to play a little joke. Very quietly, so as not to disturb the man, the minister said to his congregation, "All of you who want to go to heaven, please stand." Without any hesitation, the whole congregation—except for the sleeper—rose to their feet.

After they were all seated, the minister said, "Anyone who wishes to go to hell, please STAND UP!" Startled out of a sound sleep, the man leapt to his feet. The minister asked the man why he was standing. "I'm not sure, Reverend," the man replied. "But since you're the only other one on his feet, I guess we're in this together."

No one wants to be caught napping when it comes to our spiritual journey. We all want to do what we can to grow in the grace and knowledge of our Lord Jesus, and to please him in all we do. While each of us wants to reach the eternal happiness of heaven, I am sure many of us would say, "Soon, Lord, but not yet. I have so many things I want to do before I die."

There may be a lingering suspicion in our mind that we have not yet done enough to deserve the bliss of heaven. The words of Scripture will erase any uncertainty. St. Paul assures us, "For by grace you have been saved through faith; and this is not your own doing, it is the gift of God—not of works, lest any man should boast" (Eph 2:8-9). Salvation is God's gift to us, provided we are prepared to receive it.

In his Word, the Lord assures us that he loves us so much that he could never abandon us. On the contrary, his love is so boundless that he gave us the greatest gift imaginable—the gift of himself in the Person of Jesus, that we may have eternal life (see John 3:16-17).

In order to redeem us, Jesus laid down his life and rose from the dead to share his divine life and love with those who have the capacity to receive it. We will receive his divine life in greater fullness at the time of our death. Jesus himself affirms this truth in speaking about himself as the Good Shepherd who lays down his life for his sheep: "I came that they may have life, and have it abundantly" (Jn 10:10).

THE RESURRECTION OF LAZARUS

Lazarus and his sisters, Martha and Mary, were close friends of Jesus, who often found rest and relaxation away from the crowd in their home at Bethany. The Gospel of John records a moving story in which Jesus proclaims himself "the resurrection and the life." In this account, Lazarus dies suddenly while Jesus is away. When Jesus returns to Bethany, Martha says to him:

"Lord, if you had been here, my brother would not have died. And even now I know that whatever you ask from God, God will give you." Jesus said to her, "Your brother will rise again." Martha said to him, "I know that he will rise again in the resurrection at the last day." Jesus said to her, "I am the resurrection and the life; he who

believes in me, though he die, yet shall he live, and whoever lives and believes in me shall never die. Do you
believe this?" She said to him, "Yes, Lord; I believe that
you are the Christ, the Son of God, he who is coming
into the world."   **John 11:21-24**

Jesus was moved by the faith he found in Mary and
Martha—even the faltering faith that made them hesitate to
roll the stone away from their brother's grave for fear of the
stench. But Jesus' love for Lazarus and his power as the
Son of God were both demonstrated that day, for Jesus
raised Lazarus from the dead. By his own resurrection we
have all been given new life. We can face death willingly,
with anticipation, for we know that we will one day be
raised to *eternal* glory!

JESUS RAISES US TO ETERNAL LIFE

Jesus came into the world to restore our broken relationship with God. By his passion and death, Jesus expiated our
sinfulness; by his resurrection he restored our potential to
receive his divine life and love. St. Paul is always eloquent
when he speaks about the resurrection of Jesus. He also
explains how the resurrection made it possible for us to
share in the Lord's divine life.

Do you not know that all of us who have been baptized
into Christ Jesus were baptized into his death? We were
buried therefore with him by baptism into death, so that
as Christ was raised from the dead by the glory of the
Father, we too might walk in newness of life. For if we
have been united with him in a death like his, we shall
certainly be united with him in a resurrection like his.
                                        Romans 6:3-5

At our baptism the Lord shared his glorified, risen life with us so that "we, too, might live in the newness of life." To keep us aware of the divine indwelling, Paul asks us a rather rhetorical question: "Do you not know that you are God's temple and that God's Spirit dwells in you?" (1 Cor 3:16). Our union with God is one of the tremendous fruits made possible by the resurrection of Jesus.

Another fruit of the death and resurrection of Jesus is stated very briefly in Scripture, but it extends to every human being: "Where sin increased, grace abounded all the more" (Rom 5:20). How delighted St. Paul was to share in the Lord's divine life: "It is no longer I who live, but Christ who lives in me" (Gal 2:20).

Impelled by his infinite love, Jesus was willing to lay down his life for us in order to redeem us. In a few words he affirms his love: "Greater love has no man than this, that a man lay down his life for his friends" (Jn 15:13). Love is always eager and anxious to please the person loved. Love always responds to all the needs of the beloved.

If this is true of human love, how much truer is it of the unbounded love of God? Jesus' love for us could not be satisfied until he could meet all our needs. Could there be a greater need than our redemption?

In our unredeemed state, it was impossible for us to receive Jesus' love and life. By his resurrection, he enabled us to become partakers of his life and love, at least partially in this life and in a much fuller way when he calls us to himself at the time of our death.

"RESURRECTED CHRISTIANS"

Any time St. Paul preached or wrote about the Resurrection of Jesus, he became most eloquent and stated categorically, "If Christ has not been raised, your faith is futile and you are still in your sins" (1 Cor 15:17). And again, "Who was put to death for our trespasses and raised for our justification" (Rom 4:25). For centuries the Resurrection had tremendous significance for all Christians as they rejoiced in its fruits and the new life it imparted to them.

As time passes it is not uncommon that one phase of Christian spirituality and teaching seems to be emphasized, while another phase becomes less important to some people and is mentioned less frequently. (This does not represent the Church's doctrine, which is constant and unchanging.) This was the fate of the great significance of the Resurrection in our devotional life.

In his book *The Resurrection, A Bible Study* (1960), Fr. F.X. Durrwell writes: "Christ's work of redemption was seen as consisting in his incarnation, his life and his death on the cross."[1] For some time when the Resurrection was mentioned, it was primarily to prove the divinity of Jesus or to show his triumph over his enemies. In his scholarly work, Fr. Durrwell set the pace for a more positive view of the Resurrection and revived a vision of the fruits of the Resurrection of Jesus and our own resurrection by emphasizing our personal relationship with the risen Jesus. Looking forward to a renewed emphasis on the Resurrection in our day, he writes: "In the history of the Church's spirituality, the new realization of the Resurrection will undoubtedly come to be seen as the chief event of our day."

The Second Vatican Council, recalling the early Church's understanding of the Resurrection, reiterated its teaching that the Resurrection must be central to Christian spirituality. The Council urges us into a more personal relationship with the resurrected Jesus, a bond that is motivated by love.

Our own resurrection begins at the time of our baptism;

we become the temple of God. We receive his divine life as a tiny seed which we are to nurture by striving to become more and more receptive to the Lord throughout our earthly sojourn. The Lord will share his divine life with us more fully when we leave this earth to be with him for all eternity. We are not merely "Crucifixion Christians," dwelling solely on the passion and death of Jesus, but we are "Resurrection Christians" rejoicing in the privileged union we share with the Lord.

WE NEED NOT FEAR DEATH

Many people at some time in their lives have thought of death as a violent wrenching of the soul from the body as it takes its lone flight to the judgment seat of God. This idea naturally fills us with a great dread and fear of death.

There is a more comforting and consoling way to envision death. When we were baptized, Jesus came to live with us and within us. He promised that he would never leave us orphans, but would be with us forever. Because of our human limitations, however, we are not capable of receiving his divine life in all its fullness. We have to wait until we are called to our eternal reward to enjoy it more fully.

When I was a child, it was a family custom to plant potatoes in our little garden on Good Friday, regardless of the temperature or weather conditions. My mother used this occasion to inculcate a simple, but effective, lesson in faith. She explained that the seed potato would rest in the dark earth for some time before it would sprout and eventually produce a harvest, just as Jesus rested in the tomb for three days before he rose to share his divine life with us.

As we spend time in reflection and wordless prayer, Jesus will give us a deeper insight into the unique blessing and fruit of his Resurrection. Since he loves us and wants to be with us and within us, he gave us the capacity to receive his risen, exalted life, but only to a limited degree since we are hampered by our human bodies. Nonetheless, he wants us to be with him that he might share his divine life more fully with us. To do so, we must leave our human bodies here on earth and let him take us into the eternal peace and joy he promised. Death is not a lonely experience when we realize that Jesus never leaves us, but is with us always as he promised.

Even though our faith assures us that we will rise with Jesus who is our resurrection and our life, some fears and anxieties about death may still lurk within us. Once again Jesus tries to assure us of our rising with him and of the eternal bliss awaiting us in heaven:

> Let not your hearts be troubled; believe in God, believe also in me. In my Father's house are many rooms; if it were not so, would I have told you that I go to prepare a place for you? And when I go and prepare a place for you, I will come again and will take you to myself, that where I am you may be also. **John 14:1-3**

How comforting and consoling is this reassurance that Jesus gives us! St. Paul pondered frequently the promise of Jesus as he preached the doctrine of the Resurrection in season and out of season. He rejoiced to proclaim:

> When the perishable puts on the imperishable, and the mortal puts on immortality, then shall come to pass the saying that is written:
> "Death is swallowed up in victory."
> "O death, where is thy victory?
> O death, where is thy sting?" **1 Corinthians 15:54-55**

THE ASSUMPTION OF MARY

From the cross, Jesus gave us his Mother as our model and companion. When we reflect on our own resurrection, she is a special model for us. As we pray the Fourth Glorious Mystery of the Rosary, the Assumption of Mary into Heaven, we begin to realize how much Mary longed for that day when she would be reunited with her Son. The profound love she had for Jesus and her separation from him made these years of waiting a lonely exile for her. Even though her death or dormition is different from our death and rising, it does give us great hope.

As we reflect on her longing, her assumption into heaven and her joy in being reunited with her Son, we will be moved to implore that through her powerful intercession, we will be freed from the fear of death and will experience instead a great longing to be united with her and her Son in heaven for all eternity. When we ask Mary to "pray for us sinners now and at the hour of our death," we can be assured that our prayer is heard and will be answered.

❦

For Reflection

Before we begin a review of our convictions about death and resurrection, we would do well to recall once again the words of Jesus: "I am the resurrection and the life; he who believes in me, though he die, yet shall he live, and whoever lives and believes in me shall never die" (Jn 11:25). Ask yourself:

- Am I convinced that my death is the doorway into heaven and that Jesus will be with me to fill me with his divine life and love for all eternity?

- My resurrection began at my baptism when I first received the Lord's life and love. Do I pray for an increase of his life and love as a preparation for my own death?

- Do I ask Mary to obtain for me a freedom from the fear of death and a longing, as she had, to be reunited with her Son?

- Do I concentrate as I say, "Pray for us sinners now and at the hour of our death"?

- Do I thank the Lord daily for his redeeming love which makes our own resurrection possible?

CHAPTER SIXTEEN

"Do You Believe This?"

THROUGHOUT HIS SOJOURN ON EARTH, Jesus pleaded again and again for faith in himself as well as in all the truths he was proclaiming. When he found genuine faith, he was greatly pleased. How often he said to those who came asking for a special favor or healing, "Your faith has saved you." On the other hand, when faith in him was lacking, he was obviously deeply disappointed, because those who did not believe were depriving themselves of the blessings he wanted to give them.

The people of Nazareth, his native city, refused to believe in him. They rejected him and his teaching. Scripture relates how tragic was this rejection. "And they took offense at him.... And he did not do many mighty works there, because of their unbelief" (Mt 13:57-58).

At another time when Jesus was teaching and healing, he paused to thank and praise the Father for all those who did believe and trusted in him. Among the Jews it was not the leaders but the simple, humble people who believed in him and were disposed to listen to him with all their hearts. Jesus joyously exclaimed:

I thank thee, Father, Lord of heaven and earth, that thou hast hidden these things from the wise and understanding and revealed them to babes. **Matthew 11:25**

A childlike, humble attitude makes us open and receptive to God's gift of faith. As we journey down the roadway of life, there are many occasions when Jesus might ask us about our faith and trust in him: "Do you believe that I can do this?" or "Do you believe that I love you enough to want to do this for you?"

MARTHA MEETS JESUS

When Lazarus, the brother of Martha and Mary, became ill and died, Jesus was not in that area. When he did come to Bethany four days later, Martha chided him rather severely: "Lord, if you had been here, my brother would not have died" (Jn 11:21). Jesus assured her that her brother would rise again:

> I am the resurrection and the life; he who believes in me, though he die, yet shall he live, and whoever lives and believes in me shall never die.   **John 11:25**

Jesus then turned to Martha and asked her a direct question: "Do you believe this?" Martha's reply was a sincere act of faith: "Yes, Lord; I believe that you are the Christ, the Son of God, he who is coming into the world" (Jn 11:25-27). The word *believe* is found four times in three verses. This repetition places great emphasis on the necessity of faith.

The direct question of Jesus to Martha could have caused her some difficulty, were it not for her vibrant faith. At that time there were not many clear notions about the Resurrection. Many people had vague ideas about life hereafter. Some even denied the possibility of rising again. They did not yet have the Christian understanding and teaching about the Resurrection and eternal life that we enjoy.

Martha believed in the divinity of Jesus as the Messiah; hence, she believed he was trustworthy and his teachings were credible. Without hesitation she professed her faith in Jesus and all his teachings.

Jesus addresses that same question to us: "Do you believe this?" Are we deeply convinced that we will rise again with him? Do we ever doubt or hesitate, wondering if we are included in his promise? Do we ask ourselves if we have accomplished enough good in life to deserve to rise with him? In brief, is our faith in Jesus sufficiently firm to generate a trust and confidence in his love for us that we will arise to be happy with him for all eternity?

RESPONDING WITH GENUINE FAITH

Genuine faith engenders trust and confidence. If we have faith in a certain person, we will also trust that person. If we have faith in the Lord, we will have trust and confidence in him, enabling us to be open and receptive to whatever he may ask of us. This degree of faith empowers the Lord to work wonders in us.

Faith is a gift God implants within us and nurtures through the Holy Spirit as he dwells within us, his special temple. God does not force his divine gifts upon us but offers them and then waits for us to accept and use them for growth in our spiritual lives.

The Lord expects us to nurture and strengthen the gift of faith which is implanted in us as a tiny seed. As we strive to exercise our gift of faith at all times and in all circumstances, our faith will increase and mature. As we step out in faith, the Holy Spirit will strengthen our trust and confidence in God, which will also be a source of great peace and joy for us.

Levels of faith. Faith is often classified on three different levels or degrees.

The first level of faith is an intellectual assent to a truth which we cannot understand but one which has sufficient rationale to warrant our belief. The mystery of the Blessed Trinity is one example. It is a credible, revealed truth that is beyond our comprehension, yet is still plausible. Intellectual faith is the first and lowest level of faith.

The second level of faith is known as the faith of commitment. This level of faith is vibrant enough to enable us to commit ourselves to a special calling, program or project. Every good marriage, and also the vowed life, is based on this faith of commitment.

The next and highest level of faith is called the faith of expectancy. When we reach this degree of faith, we feel, know, believe and trust that God is acting in every situation in our lives. We are convinced that the Lord cares for us and loves us so much that everything that happens in our lives is for our good even though we may not recognize it at the time. St. Augustine assures us that God would never permit anything to happen in our life from which he cannot draw some good. This is the level of faith to which we are called.

As we pray with faith, hope and confidence, we will accept God as the central and first priority in our lives. We will then live this faith of expectancy which is most pleasing to the Lord. When we live with an expectant faith, our trust and confidence in God will increase and mature. Our faith will make us receptive to his divine influence and enable him to accomplish great things in our lives.

EXAMPLES OF FAITH IN SCRIPTURE

Scripture records many instances of God's divine power operating in those people who had faith in him. The faith of blind Bartimaeus provided the needed catalyst for his healing (Mk 10:52). In the Gospel of Matthew, two other blind men are healed according to their faith (Mt 9:28). On other occasions, when such faith was lacking, Jesus did not work many miracles because of their unbelief (Mt 13:58). This is equally true in our own lives. If we believe and trust in the Lord's mercy and compassion, he will forgive all our sinfulness. Our faith assures us that since he loves us with an infinite love, he longs to forgive us more than we could ever want it ourselves. The following are two passages in which we see examples of this truth in greater detail.

Jesus and the sinful woman. When a certain Pharisee invited Jesus to dine in his house, a sinful woman came in and went directly to where Jesus was reclining. As she wept bitterly, her tears wet the feet of Jesus, and she dried them with her hair. Recognizing her faith, humility and sorrow, Jesus assured her, "Your sins are forgiven.... Your faith has saved you; go in peace" (Lk 7:48-50).

This woman had a strong faith in Jesus. Even though she risked humiliation and ridicule, she overcame all of this—so deep was her faith and trust that Jesus would heal her.

In contrast, Simon, the Pharisee who criticized this woman for her actions, was a self-righteous person who did not believe he needed any forgiveness. Jesus pointed out his hypocrisy by contrasting Simon's behavior with that of the disreputable woman:

> Do you see this woman? I entered your house, you gave me no water for my feet, but she has wet my feet with her tears and wiped them with her hair. You gave me no

kiss, but from the time I came in she has not ceased to kiss my feet. You did not anoint my head with oil, but she has anointed my feet with ointment. Therefore I tell you, her sins, which are many, are forgiven, for she loved much; but he who is forgiven little, loves little.

Luke 7:44-47

When we both humbly and sincerely acknowledge our sinfulness before the Lord, we can be certain that when we turn to Jesus and implore his forgiveness and healing, we will hear those same words: "Your sins are forgiven.... Your faith has saved you; go in peace" (Lk 7:48-50). We may also hear Jesus ask, "Do you believe this?"

Centurion's servant. In his Gospel, St. Luke records the account of a centurion, a Gentile, who overcame his pride and asked Jesus, a Jew, to heal his dying servant. It took great courage and humility for the official to ask this favor of Jesus, yet he believed that Jesus was compassionate and would be sympathetic to his request.

Jesus was pleased to learn of the man's loving concern for his servant, since servants could be bought for a mere pittance at that time. By coming to Jesus for the good of another, the centurion manifested his love of neighbor. Jesus was amazed at the man's expression of faith. "I tell you, not even in Israel have I found such great faith" (Lk 7:9). His servant was healed at that very hour.

APPROACH GOD WITH FAITH

These episodes in Scripture reveal how pleased Jesus was to find faith, and how eager he was to reward it. As we ponder the Lord's response to the faith of these people who came to him, our own faith and trust in him will become more vibrant and dynamic in all the circumstances we face in life.

When the Lord asks us, "Do you believe this?" may we respond with the same conviction that Martha had: "Yes, Lord; I believe that you are the Christ, the Son of God, he who is coming into the world" (Jn 11:27).

⁂

For Reflection

Jesus may startle us when he asks us directly, "Do you believe this?" We want to believe and hope that we will rise with him, but we may have some doubts and misgivings stirring within us. A reflective review of our faith will bolster our convictions and bring us greater peace. Ask yourself:

- Does my faith in the Lord's divine promise enable me to trust him implicitly, especially when the fear of death arises within me?

- Do I find great reassurance and peace in the Lord's words: "I will come again and will take you to myself, that where I am you may be also" (Jn 14:3)?

- Do I frequently thank the Lord for redeeming me by his death on the cross and making it possible for me to be united with him for all eternity?

- Do I reflect as I pray so very often: "Holy Mary, Mother of God, pray for us sinners now and at the hour of our death"?

NOTES

Introduction

1. John Paul II, *Prayers and Devotions from Pope John Paul II* (New York: Viking Penguin, 1994), 103-4.

THREE
"Who Do You Say That I Am?"

1. Wendy Mary Beckett, *Simple Prayer* (Cornwall: Clergy Preview, February 1978).

SEVEN
"What Do You Want Me to Do for You?"

1. Constitution on the Sacred Liturgy, par 7.

NINE
"Who Is My Mother?"

1. R.A. Shepherd, *The Religious Poems of Richard Crashaw* (St. Louis: Herder, 1979).

FIFTEEN
"I Am the Resurrection and the Life."

1. F.X. Durrwell, *The Resurrection, A Bible Study* (New York: Sheed and Ward, 1960), foreword.